# REVIVE

## A HEART READY FOR REVIVAL

# US

## ROBBY GALLATY

Lifeway Press®
Brentwood, Tennessee

## EDITORIAL TEAM

Cynthia Hopkins
*Writer*

Reid Patton
*Senior Editor*

Stephanie Cross
*Associate Editor*

Jon Rodda
*Art Director*

Tyler Quillet
*Managing Editor*

Joel Polk
*Publisher, Small Group Publishing*

John Paul Basham
*Director, Adult Ministry Publishing*

Published by Lifeway Press® • © 2023 Robby Gallaty

No part of this book may be reproduced or transmitted in any form or by any means, electronic or mechanical, including photocopying and recording, or by any information storage or retrieval system, except as may be expressly permitted in writing by the publisher. Requests for permission should be addressed in writing to Lifeway Press®; 200 Powell Place, Suite 100; Brentwood, TN 37027-7707.

ISBN 978-1-4300-9277-3 • Item 005847233

Dewey decimal classification: 269.24
Subject headings: REVIVALS \ EVANGELISTIC WORK \ RELIGIOUS AWAKENING

Unless otherwise noted, all Scripture quotations are taken from the Christian Standard Bible®, Copyright © 2017 by Holman Bible Publishers. Used by permission. Christian Standard Bible® and CSB® are federally registered trademarks of Holman Bible Publishers.

To order additional copies of this resource, write to Lifeway Resources Customer Service; 200 Powell Place, Suite 100; Brentwood, TN 37027-7707; fax 615-251-5933; call toll free 800-458-2772; order online at lifeway.com; email orderentry@lifeway.com.

*Printed in the United States of America*

Adult Ministry Publishing • Lifeway Resources
200 Powell Place, Suite 100 • Brentwood, TN 37027-7707

# CONTENTS

# ABOUT THE AUTHOR

Robby is the Senior Pastor of Long Hollow Baptist Church in Hendersonville, TN. He was radically saved from a life of drug addiction on November 12, 2002. In 2008, he formed Replicate Ministries to equip and train men and women to be disciples who make disciples. He is also the author of multiple books.

# HOW TO USE THIS STUDY

This Bible study provides a guided process for individuals and small groups to experience revival. Six sessions of study work through the process of personal and spiritual revival. Through the study we hope and pray that God will make our hearts ready for revival.

## GROUP STUDY

Regardless of what day of the week your group meets, each session of content begins with the group session. Each group session uses the following format to facilitate simple yet meaningful interaction among group members and with God's Word.

## START

The group session will begin with a few questions designed to help you introduce the session's topic of study and encourage everyone to engage with the study.

## WATCH

This space provides Robby's teaching outline as well as blank space to take notes as you watch the video teaching. Codes to access the teaching videos are included with your purchase of this book and can be found on the insert located at the back of this book.

## DISCUSS

This section is the main component of the group session. The questions provided are designed to facilitate the group study of the session's topic. The goal is to better understand the process of spiritual revival and begin to see it in your life and church.

## PERSONAL STUDY

Three days of personal study are provided after each group session to help individuals think biblically about the session's topic. With biblical teaching and introspective questions, these lessons challenge individuals to grow in their understanding of God's Word and to respond in faith and obedience.

## PERSONAL BIBLE STUDY 1 AND 2

The group and personal studies are complementary. These studies are meant to deepen your understanding of the revival and give you more concentrated time to reflect upon and apply what you learned in the group session.

## GOING DEEPER

The personal study section ends with a guided prayer activity where you're spending time alone with God in silence and solitude to hear His voice more clearly. Being silent before God prepares us to hear from God.

## LEADER GUIDE

A cutout leader guide for each session is provided on pages 128–142, which highlights key points from each session and offers helpful considerations for leading a group discussion. Additionally, you'll find tips for helping you lead a small group.

Revive Us

SESSION 1

# DEFINING

# GROUP STUDY

## START

*Welcome everyone to session 1, "Defining."*

> Ask participants to introduce themselves. As they do, invite them to share one reason why they decided to join this study on the topic of revival.

> Have you ever experienced a revival of some sort? For example, maybe you experienced a personal revival of commitment to your job, marriage, friendship, or God. Or maybe it was a revival that spread beyond yourself—in your home, workplace, church, or community. Explain.

We all know what it is like for something that started off as exciting and fulfilling in our lives to become dull and uninspiring. When what was once a *get to* becomes a *have to* it's tough—especially when it involves an area of life that is essential to living in the best possible way.

This truth applies no where else more than in our relationship with the Lord. A relationship with the Lord is the ultimate reality—absolutely essential to everything else in our lives. That's true both personally and communally. So if we are going to move forward in faith, we can't simply know we need to change—we must experience change. We need God to revive us. We'll begin our study by taking a look at what that really means.

> How would you define spiritual revival?

> Do you have an expectation for spiritual revival? Why or why not?

> *To prepare for video session 1, pray that God will help each person understand and apply this truth:*

> Revival is available to all who seek God's presence.

# WATCH

*Use these statements to follow along as you watch video session 1.*

Revival is a heightened awareness of the presence of God.

**EXODUS 33:18**

Before we can have this intimacy with God we have to know Him personally.

**PSALM 46:10**

Before we can experience revival we must know Jesus.

**JOHN 1:14**

To access the teaching sessions,
use the instructions in the back
of your Bible study book.

# DISCUSS

*Use these questions and prompts to discuss the video teaching.*

Robby said, *You have as much of God as you want in your life, and there is so much more.* How does that statement hit you personally?

We learned a few ways to define revival in today's video teaching:

- To breathe life into something that's either dead or dormant
- To give strength or power to something
- Simply Jesus
- A heightened awareness of the presence of God

Which of these definitions stand out to you the most right now? Why?

Is it possible for you see that outcome become a reality in your life? If so, how can it take place?

What are some ways well meaning believers and/or churches might try to work to manufacture revival? How do we discern whether revival is from God or manufactured?

In our very best human efforts, we cannot bring about true revival—not personally and not corporately. God Himself brings about revival. He accelerates His work on earth by igniting the hearts of His people through His Holy Spirit.

Since God brings about revival, does that mean we can just sit back and wait for it to happen? Why not?

Read Exodus 33:1-6. What was the spiritual condition of Israel? What did they need?

Read Exodus 33:18-19. Is it strange to you that Moses said, "Let me see your glory," not "Let us see your glory"? Why would Moses pray for personal revival before corporate revival?

Robby's story about seeking God for revival did not start with prayers for revival in his church, community, and world. It didn't even start with prayers for revival in his home. It started with prayers for God to revive *him*. He explained, *Christianity is not just following Jesus to get a treasure; Jesus actually is the treasure. Christianity is not adding Jesus to an already full life; Jesus becomes your life.*

How can we know whether we're following Jesus to get a treasure or to know Him as our treasure? How can you know whether you are adding Jesus to your life or inviting Him to be your life?

Look again at Exodus 33:19. Based on God's answer to Moses, what happens when you want to see God's glory more than anything else?

Exodus 33:11 gives some insight about Moses's request and God's answer to that request. Moses was God's friend—*the Lord would speak with Moses face to face, just as a man speaks with his friend.* We also need to know the Lord personally.

Read Psalm 46:10. What do we need to do to know Jesus personally? What does it look like practically to stop fighting and know He is God?

# CLOSE IN PRAYER

*Prayer Requests*

_____

_____

_____

# A Clear Vision

When you hear the word *revival* what comes to mind? Maybe you associate the word with a church service that takes place under a big tent with fiery preaching. You may think of revivals as spiritual movements that have occurred in other places but never as part of your own personal experience. Maybe you think about a time in your life when your faith had grown stale but was suddenly awakened to become fresh and new. Or maybe you think in terms of the word's explicit meaning: "restoration to life, consciousness, vigor, strength."[1]

The truth is, the word *revival* has many connotations—and those meanings aren't necessarily *wrong*. The problem comes when our understanding is limited to a certain way we have learned about or experienced revival. We might begin to think revival is a spiritual outcome we can produce.

It's not.

True biblical revival isn't something we can program into church or personal life. It is different than organizing a campaign. One is worked up, the other is sent down. Revival is God coming down.

> **Read the following passages. Record what happened when God showed up.**
>
> Genesis 17:1–4
>
> Exodus 3:1–10
>
> Ezekiel 1:28–2:4

*One encounter with the living God
can change your life forever.*

When we encounter God, three things happen—we get a right view of God, a right view of self, and a heart for the world. It happened with Abraham, Moses, and Ezekiel. Let's look now to see how it happened with Isaiah.

# LOOK UPWARD

## A Correct Understanding of God

**Read Isaiah 6:1-8. Describe how Isaiah saw the Lord in verses 1-4.**

**What are the implications of serving a holy God?**

To say God is holy means God is perfect and totally set apart from all other beings. No one is like God. He is separated from sin and sinners; He is without equal.

In this passage, Isaiah found himself swept into the presence of the living God. He found himself face to face with the one true and holy God seated on a high and lofty throne. Note the symbolism the vision uses to reveal a correct understanding of who God is:

**AUTHORITY:** "I saw the Lord seated" (v. 1)

**MAJESTY:** "on a . . . throne" (v. 1)

**WORTH:** "high and lofty" (v. 1)

**GLORY:** "the hem of His robe filled the temple" (v. 1)

**PRESENCE:** "the temple was filled with smoke" (v. 4)

The vision of God Isaiah received speaks both to God's holiness and His unrivaled sovereignty. He is not a helpless deity on a paper-mache throne shaking His head in disbelief because He can't get His people to cooperate with Him. No, God is doing exactly what He planned to do before the world began. And He is doing it well.

**Why might we struggle to have a correct understanding of God's unrivaled sovereignty in our lives?**

Many don't know God because they have never encountered God. He is the sovereign Lord over the universe—He always has been and always will be.

Is He Lord over your life? Is He calling the shots? Are you doing things His way? Is He the center of your life? That only happens when you get a true glimpse of God.

*Your greatest need is a clear vision of who
God is in the person of Jesus Christ.*

## LOOK INWARD

### An Honest Assessment of Self

**Reread Isaiah 6:5. How did Isaiah respond to this clear vision of God?**

**Why do we need a correct view of God to have a correct view of self?**

Until Isaiah saw God for who He is, he couldn't see himself for what he was. Being in God's presence helped Isaiah see his unworthiness. Isaiah's cry, "I am ruined," really means, *I am being unmade.* The holiness of God not only means you might die, but it also means you should die; it presents a problem of forgiveness.

**If Isaiah's encounter with God ended with the words in verse 5 alone, why would God still be worthy of our worship and praise?**

Because God is holy, we are responsible to Him for every sinful action, every careless word, and every evil thought. Seeing who God is causes us to realize who we are, which is exactly what happened to Isaiah.

Notice that Isaiah didn't say, "Woe is everybody else." He cried out, "Woe is me" (v. 5). He realized the wickedness of his heart. He knew the pride in his life. He understood the immorality in his mind.

**Why is it sometimes easier for us to point out the sin in other people's lives than it is to see our own?**

**Why is it wrong to decide who we are before God by comparing ourselves to other people?**

Human nature presents obstacles to seeing ourselves correctly. We don't want to acknowledge how bad we are—we'd rather point out how bad other people are. We do not see ourselves as *ruined*. We don't believe we are unclean. We think we're not that bad. A clear vision of God gives us a clear vision of ourselves.

**Can revival take place without an honest self-assessment? Explain.**

**Read 1 John 1:7-10. In light of the holiness of God, what honest self-assessment do we each need to make?**

Revival starts individually. When you stand before God, He will not compare you to your spouse, your parents, your coworkers, your neighbors, or your friends. He will compare you to His Son, who is the epitome of perfection.

**Reread verses 6-7. Where do we see the gospel in these verses?**

What honest self-assessment could Isaiah make when this event took place?

God had every right to destroy Isaiah, but He saved him. The only way a sinful human being can come into the presence of a holy God is to be cleansed of all unrighteousness. This is why Jesus is the cornerstone of the Christian life. He is the only One who can save us from our sins—and He does! You are more sinful than you ever dared to believe and more loved by God than you ever dared to hope.

---

A PRINCIPLE FOR PERSONAL REVIVAL

*If you cover your sin, God will uncover it. But if you uncover or confess your sin, God will cover it with the blood of His Son Jesus.*

---

# LOOK OUTWARD

## A Clear Picture of the Mission

Read Isaiah 6:8. How did Isaiah respond to the clear vision of God and himself that he received?

Has true revival taken place if it does not result in missional living? Why?

The type of forgiveness Isaiah received and we receive demands a response. While Isaiah's lips were still burning from the holiness that set him free, he cried, "Here I am. Send me" (v. 8). Isaiah had seen and felt the mercy of God, and it changed his entire life.

**When Jesus is Lord of your life, you'll go wherever He sends you and do whatever He asks you. What is your gut reaction to that statement? How does it scare you? How does it excite you?**

Because it is the Lord's responsibility to protect us, we don't have to worry about a thing—we just have to fix our eyes on Jesus, with a clear picture of His mission. If someone does us harm, He will settle the score. His job is to care for us, feed us, clothe us, and provide for our needs. He will lead us, guide us, and instruct us along the way.

**How would your life change if you truly walked in full assurance of the following statement: *Because God's concern is to protect and direct my way, my only concern is to know and do God's will?***

True revival happens when we gain a right view of God, a right view of self, and a heart for the world. Knowing who God is calls us into action for His name. Studying God's character is not an abstract discipline for a select group of gifted Christians but the responsibility of every believer. When we see who God is, we must respond. We must go, full and filled from the forgiveness we have received in Jesus Christ.

We don't experience revival because we've been content to live without it. We need a fresh vision of God. He can do more in a moment than any man, machine, or method can mass-produce in a lifetime. Are you ready?

*You have as much of God as you want in your life—and there is so much more.*

1. "Revival," in *The New Dictionary of Cultural Literacy* (Boston, MA: Houghton Mifflin Harcourt Publishing, 2005), https://www.dictionary.com/browse/revival.

# An Outpouring of Power

We are taught to believe anything is possible with determination and positivity. A multitude of popular cultural maxims express that belief and seek to motivate us—*If you can dream it, you can achieve it. Work hard and make it happen. Believe in yourself.*

Those ideas carry some truth. We certainly should dream new possibilities, work hard, and believe we can enact change. There is value in setting our minds to goals and working hard to achieve them. At the same time, though, immense danger comes when we ignore the greater truth: in and of ourselves, we are powerless.

**Read Ephesians 2:1–5. How can we know we are powerless to bring about spiritual change in our lives?**

We need to be realistic about our spiritual capacity. Becoming a Christian requires nothing less than fully confronting the fact that we are spiritually dead and completely unable to do anything to better our spiritual condition.

**Name a situation where you work hard to strategize human solutions instead of inviting the Lord to enact His power.**

To truly understand revival, we need a reminder of Christ's greatness and our poverty, His power and our weakness, His ability and our ineptness.

# We Are Powerless to Bring about Revival

Read Mark 9:14-18,21-22. What does the length of time this family had suffered reveal about the power they had to overcome this affliction on their own?

This likely wasn't the first time the father had sought help for his child. His situation was probably similar to the woman who had the issue of blood and had spent a lot of money visiting many physicians but gained no relief (Mark 5:21-43).

The fundamental problem here was that the child couldn't help himself; he could do nothing to rid himself of the evil spirit. He was completely incapable of stifling the convulsions and keeping himself from heading straight toward the fire or water. His parents were similarly incapable. And, as the disciples quickly learned, they also lacked the power needed to change the boy's life.

When have you faced a situation where you realized you were powerless to bring about change in your own strength? How did you respond?

Belief in the dreams of a better life and the hard work and determination to make it happen would never be enough. If left to human ingenuity and strength, the child's situation was completely hopeless—and so is ours.

*We will never experience any real power if we trust in ourselves.*

What are some ways we might be tempted to seek revival through human strength instead of God's power?

# We Must Rely Completely on Jesus to Experience Revival

When these events in Mark 9 occurred, Jesus had just come off a true mountain top experience with three of His disciples (vv. 1-13). As Jesus was transfigured, God revealed the fullness of His power. Then they came down the mountain and walked into a dumpster fire. People were yelling and accusing the other disciples of being powerless. Jesus stepped into the situation and took charge.

> **Read Mark 9:19-20. What do these verses teach you about Christ's heart for people?**

> **Why couldn't the disciples do anything to change the boy's situation? Jesus knew the disciples were powerless people. So why was He upset that they hadn't helped the boy receive new life?**

> **Read Mark 9:28-29. What do Jesus's words, "This kind can come out by nothing but prayer," teach you about how revival takes place?**

It would be a mistake to take Jesus's words as some sort of formulaic, demon-busting one-two punch. Jesus wasn't giving the disciples a formula but was explaining how such unmistakable spiritual power came forth—in complete and humble dependence on God, expressed through urgent and serious prayer.

*Spiritual battles must be fought by spiritual means.*

Instead of trusting in God's power, the disciples had shifted their faith to them-selves. That was foolish—it always is. God's work must be done in God's power. On our own, we can't fix the brokenness we see. Only through the power and love of Christ will true change come about. We will only experience the power and love of Christ to bring revival if we rely on Him completely.

**What behaviors might show a person is desperately dependent on Jesus's power to enact change?**

Jesus wasn't giving the disciples a formula for revival. Salvation is a gift of grace, not works—and so is every bit of our spiritual growth from that point forward. Still, we have a choice about whether we will depend on the Lord to produce spiritual renewal in us or, like the disciples in Mark 9, shift our faith to our own abilities.

Prayer and fasting indicate people who desperately depend on God to work in and through them. Based on Jesus's words in verses 19 and 29, this wasn't how the disciples operated here.

**Read Mark 6:7-13. How might this success have served as a hindrance to the disciples as they tried to heal the demon-possessed boy in Mark 9?**

*Our past success can be a great hindrance to God's work in the present.*

Jesus had just sent these disciples off on a citywide crusade to heal the sick and cast out demons. He had given them the power of God to pray over the most hopeless, helpless, and darkest situation and turn it around. But just a few chapters later, they could do nothing. Selfish pride and divine power cannot share the same stage.

What are some successes in church life that might make believers become prideful? How have you seen this happen?

The problem is never with God; it is always with us. Stated more plainly and personally, the barrier to revival is *you*.

## Revival Is Possible for Those Who Believe

The child couldn't heal himself. The disciples couldn't cast out the demon in their own strength. The child's father and the crowd represent a third example of inadequacy. The father couldn't believe without Jesus helping His unbelief.

> Read Mark 9:22–27. What indicates the man's disbelief? How do we often respond to God similarly in prayer?

Sometimes God chooses not to answer our prayers and petitions in the ways we desire, but this never comes from a lack of ability. The man's words, "If you can do anything" (v. 22), indicate that he doubted Jesus had the power to heal his son.

This is different than praying, God, if it is your will. When we pray, we ought to affirm and agree with God's prerogative to act according to His will. But we never have to doubt God's ability to answer our prayers.

> How did the man respond to Jesus's rebuke? How are we called to respond in similar situations?

The father immediately recognized his deficiency and sought the Lord's help. Even faith is a gift from God for those who seek Him. This is why the man cried out for help increasing his faith. Similarly, this is why the disciples pleaded, "Increase our faith" (Luke 17:5).

The child's father recognized his deficiency of faith and asked Jesus to fill what was lacking. His request stood as an example to the crowd and gives us an example as we read this account.

We are called to depend on the Lord to save us from our sin, empower us for ministry, and revive us along the way so that we might walk in ever-increasing faith. This means we should abandon attempts to muster up faith on our own and pour our efforts into seeking the Lord and pleading with Him for revival. Jesus is the only One who can truly transform our lives and our world to make us whole.

**Do you believe God can bring revival to you in this day and time? What doubt might keep you from believing that? Confess it to God and invite Him to enact revival in His power.**

**Do you believe God can bring revival in your local church? What doubt might keep you from believing that? Confess it to God and invite Him to enact revival in His power.**

**Do you believe God can bring revival in your community, country, and even around the world? What doubt might keep you from believing that? Confess it to God and invite Him to enact revival in His power.**

God doesn't call us to work harder and develop ingenious strategies so that we might change the world; He calls us to desperately trust Him to reveal His power in us, through us, and around us. Revival is possible in your life, church, community, country, and world—but it isn't up to you; it's up to Jesus. Will you believe?

*When you become a believer in Jesus, God doesn't add a burden—He adds power to live.*

# SILENCE AND SOLITUDE
## ESTABLISH A RHYTHM

If you're going to look upward, inward, and outward to receive an outpouring of God's power in your life, you're going to have to spend some time in silence and solitude before Him. Being alone or quiet may not be A normal practice for you. But when you set aside the norm for a time, you can better engage with God and grow in relationship with Him.

## FIVE MINUTES

This week, get started in the spiritual practice of silence and solitude. In the weeks to come, you'll continue establishing that new rhythm as you increase your time.

1. **Determine a time you will commit to spend time alone with the Lord each day this week.** It won't come naturally. You must be intentional to seek moments of physical solitude and silence of heart.

2. **Find a place where you can spend that time in silence and solitude.** Jesus had to climb a mountain to find solitude. You might have to go sit in your car or in your closet. But no matter what challenges you face, find that place—you need this time, and it's worth it.

3. **Read one verse to direct your thoughts to who God is, such as Psalm 46:10 or Psalm 62:5.**

4. **Be silent before the Lord for five minutes.** Silence isn't as much the absence of noise as it is an attitude of listening to God. You can be physically alone and still be distracted by world's voice. So turn off your cell phone or, better yet, don't even take it with you. Be quiet before God and invite Him to speak to your heart.

5. **At the end of that time, jot down the thoughts God impressed on you.** Use the page provided here to record them.

6. **Repeat these steps each day this week.**

*Scan athe QR code to hear guidance from Robby
about spending time in silence and solitude.*

# PREPARING

# GROUP STUDY

## START

*Welcome everyone to session 2, "Preparing." Before introducing session 2, take a few minutes to review session 1.*

Before starting the new content each week, we'll spend some time talking about insights we discovered during the previous week's personal study and time of silence and solitude. The review questions will be simple, designed to help us press into what God's Word is teaching us about revival.

> **What did you learn about revival in your study of Isaiah 6:1-8 and Mark 9:14-29?**
>
> **What stood out to you as particularly helpful as you began to establish a rhythm of silence and solitude (pages 26-27)? What was particularly challenging?**

Sitting before the Lord in silence and solitude isn't always easy or comfortable, but it is always beneficial. We engage in silence and solitude before God so that we can listen as He reveals to us the places in our lives that need His holy and loving correction.

*To prepare for video session 2, pray that God will help each person understand and apply this truth:*

> Repentance is the pavement we walk on throughout our entire sanctification process.

# WATCH

*Use these statements to follow along as you watch video session 2.*

Are you the blood clot to revival coming to your home, your church, and your community?

Repentance is change in one's mind about sin that leads to a change of action in one's life.

Three Steps to Repentance:

1. Acknowledge there is a God who knows what's best for you.

2. Confess that sin to God.

3. Return to God.

Repentance is a lifestyle.

To access the teaching sessions, use the instructions in the back of your Bible study book.

# DISCUSS

*Use these questions and prompts to discuss the video teaching.*

In the video teaching, Robby explained that he began his season of intentional silence and solitude before God when two men in his church met with him to talk to him about some of his blind spots.

> Since we are all blind to the blinds spots in our lives, what are some steps we can take to discover and address those issues?

> Read the following verses together and discuss what God's Word indicates is involved:

> Psalm 139:23-24

> Proverbs 27:17

> Galatians 6:1-2

> James 5:16

> Does it make you more excited or uncomfortable to think about taking those steps? Explain.

We learned that the Holy Spirit has an amazing ability to put His finger on the pulse of the problem in our lives if we ask Him. He does that through our study of Scripture, prayer, silence and solitude, and even through other believers.

> What was the first message of the public ministries of John the Baptist, Jesus, and Peter (Matthew 3:2; 4:17; Acts 2:38)? Why should that matter to us?

What has repentance looked like in your life to this point: an initial acknowledgment of sin and turning to faith in Jesus, a cyclical acknowledgment of need that prompts an attempt to do better, or a lifestyle of acknowledging sin and returning to God? Explain.

In the video teaching, we were asked to consider: *What is the secret sin in your life that you've been holding back from God?* God knows about it, has already forgiven it, and is waiting on you to confess it.

What does the following statement inform you about preparing for God to bring revival in your life, church, and community: *The distance between you and revival may be the distance between your knees to the floor in prayer.*

What is involved in the kind of prayer that invites God to bring personal revival?

In the session Robby spoke about the Ignatian Examen, which is an exercise of identifying consolations and desolations—things that draw you to God and things that draw you away from God during the day.

How can identifying thoughts and experiences, both good and bad, before the Lord help you practice a lifestyle of repentance?

## CLOSE IN PRAYER

*Prayer Requests*

# When God Seems Distant

Think about a time someone said or did something that hurt you. You can probably also remember a time when you hurt someone else's feelings, grieving them with your actions or words. When human relationships become strained or broken, we know it—and feel it deeply.

Until someone makes a confession or gives forgiveness, the relationship remains strained. Conversations are tense; intimacy is non-existent; and we find ourselves walking on eggshells.

**How might tensions in your earthly relationships affect your relationship with God?**

We don't often connect our relationships with others to our relationship with God, but we should because they matter. Many of us grieve the Holy Spirit through the way we treat others, and we usually aren't even aware of it. Preparing ourselves for revival begins by taking an honest inventory of the sin in our lives. If you don't know where to start, begin with your relationships.

*We limit God's power and presence in our lives when we mistreat other people.*

Read Habakkuk 1:13. Why does your sin grieve the Holy Spirit?

If you are a Christian, then God's Spirit dwells in you. But God cannot stand the presence of sin—those living conditions grieve Him. When we grieve the Holy Spirit with ongoing sin, we lose all sense of His presence, eliminate joy, limit God's power in our lives, and cease to be useful in His kingdom.

## YOUR SIN AND NEGLECT GRIEVES THE HOLY SPIRIT

Read Ephesians 4:29-32. Note the specific sins Paul mentions that grieve the Holy Spirit. For each of those relational sins, give one example.

Speech (v. 29)

Bitterness (v. 31)

Anger (v. 31)

Lack of compassion (v. 32)

Unforgiveness (v. 32)

Paul's list is not exhaustive. What are some other sins in your life that grieve the Holy Spirit?

*You can only grieve the Holy Spirit for so long*
*before He shrinks back from working in your life.*

What does Ephesians 4:30 teach you about personal revival?

Continue reading Ephesians 4:31-32. What do these verses teach you about corporate revival in the local church and the global body of Christ? How are our relationships related to grieving the Holy Spirit

Personal revival begins with a renewed sense of the Spirit's work in your life. The Spirit indwells you at salvation and never leaves you. He is also ever-present in God's church, both locally and globally. And at the very same time, His conscious presence can certainly become absent from us. Unconfessed sin always causes distance in your relationship with God.

Have you ever felt like God was distant? What caused that to happen?

How can you prepare yourself for a revival of intimacy with the Lord?

## CONFESSION IS THE DOORWAY TO RESTORATION

Read Ephesians 1:5,13. What is unconditional for all who trust in Jesus?

Read Galatians 5:1,16,22-25. According to these verses what might we miss out on if we quench the Holy Spirit?

At the moment of salvation, you are made positionally right with God for eternity. You can't do anything to change your place in God's family. You didn't earn your spot in the family. Jesus paid the price with His life on the cross of Calvary so that you could be called a son or daughter of the King. However, though our salvation is unconditional and sealed, the work of the Spirit can be quenched. He can be experienced to a lessor or greater degree. Preparing for revival and receiving from God creates space in our lives for the Spirit to manifest His presence and power.

> *When you are out of fellowship with the Father, you must confess your sin to Him.*

You don't fix yourself by trying to be better or work harder. That's not how restoration or revival happens. Instead, you must accept the love of a forgiving Father who restores you to right relationship with Him.

**Read Luke 15:3-7. Who restored what was lost, the shepherd or the sheep?**

**Read Luke 15:8-10. Who restored what was lost, the woman or the coin?**

**Read Luke 15:11-24. Who ran to enact restoration?**

> IN THE THREE LOST PARABLES, THE EMPHASIS IS ON . . .
> *the shepherd finding the sheep.*
> *the woman finding the coin.*
> *the father running to the son.*

**How do you explain why the father would run to the son in this situation?**

When the prodigal son left the father and turned his back on the family, he was still a son—even though he wasn't acting like it. If he had died in the pigpen, he would still be his father's son. The relationship is fixed, but the intimacy shifted.

**Has personal sin ever caused you to be out of fellowship with the Lord? Explain.**

**What stays the same in your relationship with God during those times? What changes?**

If we live in sin, we will still gain entrance into the Father's glory. However, we will suffer the loss of rewards in the future as well as unspeakable joy and power in the present.

**What was the son's responsibility in the act of restoration?**

**What can we learn from this restoration about our restoration with God?**

If we confess our sins, he is faithful and righteous to forgive us our sins and to cleanse us from all unrighteousness.

**1 JOHN 1:9**

**What are some reasons we might shy away from confessing our sins when we're alone with God? What about in the context of church life?**

Some of us are too ashamed to confess what we have done to the Lord. Some are too embarrassed to ask God for help. Like the father in the parable of the lost son, God is waiting for you to confess your sin so that He can restore you to fellowship with Him. He is ready to offer you a clean slate, pick you up, and put you on a path to restored intimacy. He has an amazing Spirit-filled life for you, but you have to take the initiative and confess your sin.

**Why is confession of sin a necessary part of personal revival?
Why is it a necessary part of corporate revival?**

*When you grieve the Holy Spirit, you move from God ministering through you to God ministering to you.*

Some of us have grieved the Holy Spirit by things we've said this past week. Some of us have grieved the Holy Spirit by how we've talked about people this week. Some of us have grieved the Holy Spirit by what we've posted online this week. Some of us have grieved the Spirit by how we spoke to people this week.

If we're going to experience restoration, all of us need to come before God in honest confession and repent of our grievous words, actions, attitudes, and conversations. He is waiting, ready to revive us.

# When We've Fallen Asleep

We have learned that confession is the doorway to restoration and revival (1 John 1:9). However, if we fail to sit before the Lord in silence and solitude, then we might be tempted to think of confession only as something *other* people need to do. However, confession is something *you* need to do. Corporate revival starts with you. God is trying to get your attention right now.

*Personal renewal is the road map to corporate revival.*

Can revival take place in your life apart from spending time in silence and solitude before the Lord? Why or why not?

What is the relationship between silence and confession?

## IT IS BETTER TO LISTEN THAN TO SPEAK

Read Matthew 26:31-35. What message was Jesus wanting to get across to His disciples?

**Did He get their attention with that message? How do you know?**


Jesus wanted Peter to listen; Peter just wanted to talk. Our prayer lives are often like that. We are so busy trying to tell Jesus what we want Him to do that we miss what He is saying.

**What warning does Matthew 26:31-35 offer you? What does this passage teach you about yourself?**


**How would you describe your prayer life? Circle any words that fit:**

shallow          two-sided          one-sided          selfish

rote          receptive          short

quiet          submissive          other: _____


*Prayer is a dialogue with God, not a monologue.*


**Have you ever prayed and thought, "I don't even know what to pray for," or "What should I pray in this situation?" If so, what did you do?**


**Read Romans 8:26. What does this teach you about prayer?**


You don't have to have the right words to say in prayer. God is not impressed with eloquent speech or impressive phrases. In fact, even when you are at a complete loss for words to say, the Spirit will pray *for* you. Some of the greatest prayers have no language; they are simply cries to the Lord. God hears our cries, even when they are wordless—and He answers them. But He wants us to lean in and listen.

*Our loving Father knows the language of His children's cries.*

Peter's problem was that he didn't listen to what Jesus told him. Jesus then brought Peter and the other disciples to the garden of Gethsemane.

## IT IS BETTER TO PRAY THAN TO SLEEP

**Read Matthew 26:36-46. What did Jesus want the disciples to do? Why?**

**Contrast Jesus's attitude in the garden with the attitude of His disciples.**

Jesus models for us what to do when we are facing difficult situations in life: hit your knees and ask God to work. All our battles—the ones we face as individual believers, as a church, for our children, our country, and our world—are won or lost in the garden. We prepare ourselves for revival by acknowledging our desperate need through prayer.

The disciples, though, hit their backs and fell asleep. They weren't desperate for God's help in this situation. They didn't yet recognize their desperate need. They were willing to pray, but they were weak in heart, mind, and strength.

**In this passage, who do you relate to more when you face a difficult situation: Jesus, who desperately wanted to seek the Father and do His will; or the disciples, who tried to sleep it off? Why?**

*God is looking to see who is serious in the garden.*

Can you relate to Jesus's words, "The Spirit is willing, but the flesh is weak" (v. 41)? How so?

Read John 14:13-14 and James 4:2. Why might God's people not experience revival even when they desperately need it?

Maybe you've prayed and God didn't answer the way you wanted Him to. Sometimes when that happens, we find ourselves questioning if God really hears our prayers. John 14:13-14 and James 4:2 assure us He does! Don't let past prayers that weren't answered the way you wanted keep you from praying today.

We must recognize that Jesus holds editing rights over all our prayers. Prayer is not an attempt to get God to see things from our point of view; prayer is our attempt to see things from God's point of view. Like Jesus in the garden, when we pray honestly and humbly in accordance with God's character, purpose, and ultimate glory, He will revive us.

## IT IS BETTER TO CONFESS THAN TO DENY

Three times Jesus came back to find the disciples sleeping. Peter woke up from a nap and realized Judas was coming with the guards to take Jesus away.

Read Matthew 26:47-56. How did Peter react when Jesus was arrested (see also John 18:10-11)?

What do verses 53-54 teach you that sleeping Peter had not yet learned?

In his sleepy state, Peter reacted poorly: He cut off a soldier's ear. Why did he do the wrong thing? He was sleeping instead of praying. If he had been praying, he would have been prepared to face the temptations coming his way—and he would have been better equipped to respond in faith.

Luke 22:51 tells us Jesus healed the soldier's ear. Prayerless Peter, though, continued to struggle. As the guards led Jesus to the high priest's house, Peter followed them into the courtyard at a safe distance.

**Read Luke 22:54-62. Physically, Peter was now wide awake, but how do you know he was still sound asleep spiritually?**

After falling asleep in the garden, Peter's bold declaration in Matthew 26:35 quickly fell apart. Instead of trusting Jesus, Peter leaned into his own strategies. Instead of stopping to confess his sin and acknowledge his need, he fought, he ran, and he separated himself from Jesus. In fact, while Jesus was being beaten to the point of death, Peter was denying Him in the courtyard.

*Peter failed in the courtyard*
*because he slept in the garden.*

**Read 1 John 1:8-10. What happens when we confess our sins? What happens when we don't?**

**Why does sin always compound apart from confession?**

Peter's story illuminates ours—we're not serious about prayer because we're not sick of sin. Before the rooster crowed, Peter's prayerlessness kept him unaware of the depth of his spiritual need. After the rooster crowed, Peter awakened to his desperate need. Will you?

# IT IS BETTER TO WAKE UP THAN TO MISS REVIVAL

Read Acts 1:12-14. Jesus had died, resurrected, and ascended into heaven. So what are some reasons Peter and the other disciples were committed to pray *now?*

Read Acts 2:1-8,37-41. How did God answer their prayers?

The measure of a life is not by degrees, accolades, financial position, job title, church size, or ministry excellence. No man or woman is greater than his or her prayer life. Whether we fail or succeed comes down to whether we pray—confessing our sins and acknowledging our need for God to revive us.

Read Proverbs 3:5-6. What promise is there for us when we "wake up" in prayerful confession?

*Revival starts by repenting for sleeping in the garden.*

We aren't seeing revival in our lives, churches, towns, countries, and world because we're content to live without it. Are you tired of business as usual and going through the motions? Do you yearn for more of God? Do you want to see Him revive your family and friends, your city, church, and the world?

# SILENCE AND SOLITUDE
## CONFESSION

Read Jeremiah 17:9-10. Why is it impossible for you to prepare yourself for revival without silence and solitude before God?

It is easy to think wrongly about ourselves. What we feel is not often true. But God searches and knows our hearts. So, the practice of self-examination and repentance invites God to help us know what He sees when He searches our hearts, because we can't search our hearts without His help.

Search me, God, and know my heart;
test me and know my concerns.
See if there is any offensive way in me;
lead me in the everlasting way.

**PSALM 139:23-24**

## TEN MINUTES

*This week, look to increase your time of silence and solitude to ten minutes each day, focusing on confession and repentance. Begin each day by praying Psalm 139:23-24. Listen as God reveals the sins of your heart and mind. Then confess them back to Him in repentance.*

*Use the blank page provided to record what God reveals to you.*

*Scan athe QR code to hear guidance from Robby about spending time in silence and solitude.*

SESSION 3

# RECEIVING

# GROUP STUDY

## START

*Welcome everyone to session 3, "Receiving." Before introducing session 3, take a few minutes to review session 2.*

As we did last week, we want to spend some time reviewing the previous session, personal study, and your time of silence and solitude. As we study God's Word, we're discovering what biblical revival means and how to prepare ourselves to receive it.

> **What did you learn about revival in your study of Matthew 26:31-56; Luke 15:3-24; and Ephesians 4:29-32?**
>
> **What stood out to you as you began to connect the practice of confession with silence and solitude (pages 46-47)? Is there anything particularly challenging to you about that? Why or why not?**

Personal sin gets in the way of personal revival. It's not that we need to be sinless for God to move in our lives—for one thing, that's impossible. More importantly, we don't have the power to stop God from carrying out His plans and purposes. But if we are not engaging in spiritual practices that align us with His plans and purposes, we are prone to miss them altogether. This week, we'll take a look at some spiritual disciplines that help us receive God's purpose of reviving us to new life in Him.

*To prepare for video session 3, pray that God will help each person understand and apply this truth:*

> We can't earn grace from God, but we can position ourselves to receive it more readily.

# WATCH

*Use these statements to follow along as you watch video session 3.*

We all need a place where we can meet with God.

God is always speaking to us. Are we listening?

Every great movement of God begins with not moving.

**PSALM 46:10**

To access the teaching sessions,
use the instructions in the back
of your Bible study book.

# DISCUSS

*Use these questions and prompts to discuss the video teaching.*

Before we jump into our discussion of the helps given to us in the video teaching, let's talk about our struggles with the topic in general. What keeps you from hearing from the Lord?

We learned that everything changes when God speaks, and God is always speaking! The challenge is for us to listen. Spiritual disciplines position us to hear from Him.

Do you have a place where you meet regularly with God? If so, why is that place important to you? If not, where might be a place you can go?

Read Mark 1:35-38. Where did Jesus go to pray? Why would He choose such a place?

From Jesus's reaction to the disciples who found Him there, what are some principles we can learn about silence and solitude?

The practice of spiritual disciplines works alongside the call to engage in God's kingdom work. Jesus didn't turn to His disciples and say, "Guys, can't you see I'm praying? The people can wait!" When they found Jesus, He got up from His spot and went with them to continue His ministry. After all, people were the very reason He was on earth.

At the same time, Jesus did prioritize time alone with the Father. He very intentionally got up early in the morning and went to a deserted place without telling His disciples.

In the video teaching, Robby explained that sitting with the Lord is not trying to get something from God; it is actually being with God. How does this truth help explain why Jesus was ready to re-engage with people when His disciples found Him?

How might understanding that truth impact your own spiritual practices?


Read Isaiah 57:15. Where are the two places God dwells?


Why does God dwell with those whose spirits are contrite and humble?


What connection is there between spending time in silence and solitude before the Lord and becoming a humble and contrite person?


We can't earn grace from God, but we can align ourselves in a position where we can receive God's grace more readily. We can align ourselves in a position to hear from God and when we hear from God, everything changes. That's what happened for Robby as he committed to five minutes of silence and solitude before the Lord. It grew to ten minutes, then twenty, until eventually he was spending two hours with the Lord every night. God was faithful to meet Him there.

We read Psalm 46:10 in our week 1 discussion. Let's read it again. Close your eyes and meditate on that verse in the way it was described to us in the video teaching: Be still and know I am God. Be still and know I am. Be still and know. Be still. Be.

Name one way you will choose to *be* before God this week.


# CLOSE IN PRAYER

*Prayer Requests*

_____

_____

_____

# Fasting

If God brought revival in the context of your life and church, would you be ready for it? Would your church? Why or why not?

We find ourselves in a unique scenario—globally, nationally, locally, and personally. Our world is simultaneously more connected yet more fractured and alone than ever before. We can share our thoughts and know anyone else's instantly, yet many feel more isolated and disconnected from true relationship. We need a genuine move of God in our churches, communities, country, and world.

The prophet Daniel found himself in a similar unprecedented situation: he and many of his friends were taken into a culture in need of revival. He wept over the people's love for this world. God's people got sucked into the system and culture of Babylon. In response, Daniel was moved to fast for more of God.

*God will pour out His Spirit on a people*
*who hunger for more of Him.*

## HUNGRY TO RECEIVE

Read Daniel 10:2-7. What word did Daniel use to describe fasting (v. 2)?

How is the practice of fasting tied to mourning and lament?

Eventually, the king allowed God's people to return to Israel from Babylon. He said, "You don't have to stay here any longer. You can go back to your homeland and rebuild the house of God." However, the people built homes and established themselves in the community. They got sucked into the promises, allure, and pleasures of Babylon. As a result, they didn't want to return to God.

**After three weeks of fasting, what did Daniel experience that the men with him did not?**

After pressing into God and seeking Him for three weeks, Daniel looked up and saw the Lord. Don't miss this: God wants to show up. He's not a shrewd business owner who keeps His resources to Himself. He wants to give good gifts to those who ask. He wants us to draw near to Him so He can draw near to us.

*God manifests His presence to those who look for Him.*

Only Daniel saw the angel of God. The men around him sensed something dreadful was happening, so they ran. Maybe God only wanted Daniel to receive the vision, or maybe Daniel was the only one spiritually ready to handle it.

**The men in this passage were all in the same situation but responded differently. Place a check beside any word that describes a response of someone ready to receive revival from God. Place an X beside any word that describes a response of someone not ready to receive revival from God.**

☐ desperate    ☐ satisfied    ☐ prayerful    ☐ fasting

☐ resigned    ☐ dependent    ☐ independent    ☐ broken

☐ waiting    ☐ settling    ☐ impatient    ☐ hopeful

**Now circle any of those words that describe your response to your current culture and context.**

Many of us respond to disrupting events from our sinful nature and in our own strength. As a result, we dull our spiritual senses. It's not always obvious when that happens. In fact, we can seem spiritual—to ourselves and others—when we are actually operating in our flesh. We often do this by responding with spiritual anger instead of spiritual anguish. Responding this way can cause us to miss a move of God.

Based on Daniel 10:2-7, what do you need to do to become ready to receive a fresh vision from God?

*When God lights a fire, some people stand too far away to get warm. Is that you?*

## HUMBLED TO RECEIVE.

Read Daniel 10:8-11. List words in the passage that describe Daniel as he received this vision of God.

Considering Daniel's commitment to seeking the Lord through fasting and praying, is Daniel's state of being surprising to you? Why?

When Daniel fasted and prayed for three weeks, God showed up. And when God showed up, Daniel went to his knees. He didn't stand to shout a war cry over Israel, run off in self-confidence and courage, or even sit in satisfaction that all his questions and fears were resolved. In fact, he found himself trembling, powerless and alone.

Why does a fresh vision of God bring human weakness and trembling instead of strength and courage?

For what reason could Daniel stand, even though he was weak and trembling (v. 11)?

The purpose of fasting and praying is not that we might self-actualize and realize our power and potential in the world. The purpose of fasting and praying is that we might receive a fresh vision of God, realizing His power and purpose in the world. The practice of spiritual disciplines is not self help; it is the acknowledgment of our desperate need for God's help. Receiving that help from a true vision of His holiness sends us to our knees.

What are some signs a person has received a true vision of God's holiness?

How does receiving a true vision of God move our faith beyond an intellectual exercise?

When you encounter the risen Christ, it is evident—to you and everyone else. When your life intersects with the God of the universe, it leaves a mark. The problem is, many of us would rather define a move of God than desire it. We'd rather explain it than experience it. We'd rather spectate than participate in it.

*We have adopted an intellectual faith in place of— and at the expense of—an experiential faith.*

Which resonates most personally: intellectual faith or experiential faith? What do pride and humility have to do with your faith reality?

# HELPED TO RECEIVE

Read Daniel 10:12-14. Why did the Lord's angel come to Daniel?

From the very first moment Daniel started humbly asking for a fresh vision from God, God heard his prayers. Your prayers have power. God hears your prayers and will answer them. Don't give up!

**Why did it take three weeks for Daniel to receive a fresh vision of God?**

The angel was held up for twenty-one days in the spiritual realm, but Daniel didn't stop fasting and praying—and neither should we. Instead of giving up, we need to be on guard for attacks. When the Lord moves, you should expect a counter move from Satan.

*Everything that happens in the natural realm first happens in the spiritual realm.*

We need to stop fighting a spiritual battle with natural weapons. Prayer for God's people is like oxygen for the human body.

**Because Daniel did not stop seeking the Lord, what help did the angel come to give (v. 14)?**

People who receive an outbreak of revival from God are committed to humbly praying to God. The greatest thing you can do is pray. Pray for your family. Pray for yourself. Pray for your pastor. Pray for your pastor's family. Pray for your church staff. Pray for your small group. Pray for your coworkers, neighbors, community, and country. Pray for the world. Pray for God to move. And He will! God has sent His Spirit who dwells within us, ready to help us receive revival.

**Read the following verses and record what help we receive from the Spirit when we pray.**

Acts 1:14; 2:1-4,38-41

Acts 2:42-47

Acts 4:31

*The Holy Spirit will never impose Himself on you.
He won't enter unless you welcome Him in.*

The moment you turn to Jesus in faith, the Holy Spirit comes to live inside of you. But we must not quench Him or grieve Him. You won't walk in the power of God with casual praying. You won't experience the manifestation of the Spirit of God with a discount devotional life.

Are you willing to pray until God comes? Are you willing to humble yourself and admit you've tried to live without God? Are you willing to cry out until God shows up?

# Interceding

**Who has interceded for you in some way? How did he or she do that?**

**Who do you feel compelled to intercede for now? How?**

Harriet Ross Tubman was born enslaved around 1820 on a Maryland plantation. She grew up surrounded by the cruelty of enslavers and the oppression of her enslaved brothers and sisters—and she resolved to do something about it.

After a daring escape, Harriet found freedom in the North. Her freedom was only the beginning, though. Harriet was called to make a way for others to be free. So she became a conductor on the Underground Railroad, rescuing others from the plantations where they were enslaved. In fact, Harriet Tubman set so many people free from slavery that some started calling her Moses.

You may have never thought of an intercessor in this way, but that is exactly what the word means. Intercessors stand in the gap. They put the target on their backs so that other people can move from slavery to freedom. They give their time and energy to help others.

*An intercessor is someone who stands before*
*the Lord on behalf of other people.*

Read Luke 4:18 and Romans 8:1–4. How has Jesus acted as an intercessor?

Read Galatians 5:1,13–18 and 1 Timothy 2:1–6. Since Jesus has already provided the freedom we need, why must we now intercede for each other?

# AN INTERCESSOR KNOWS GOD

**Read Genesis 18:16–19. What do you learn about Abraham's relationship with God?**

We find the first example of intercessory prayer in Genesis 18. But we see something important before that intercession took place—Abraham was known by God and seeking to know God. In verse 19 we read God's words about that: "For I have chosen him." Those words can be translated "For I have known him" or "For he is my intimate friend." God called Abraham a friend, and that's not a title you receive lightly (James 2:23).

**Who in your life would say embraces his or her calling to be God's friend? What about him or her makes you think that?**

**Do you embrace your invitation to be God's friend? What does/would that look like in your life?**

Many people hunger for spiritual vitality, but they look in all the wrong places. They wear crystals, have stones in their pockets, spend money talking to gurus, read horoscopes, or seek transcendence through any number of supposedly spiritual practices. In this, they are saying they have tried religion and want something more. For others, Christianity has become a checklist of things to do, and Sunday is simply a date on the calendar.

**Why does intercession necessitate friendship with Jesus (John 14:6)?**

The gospel requires no additions or alterations. Anything you add to the gospel—anything you add to a relationship with Jesus—is no longer Christianity. It is not friendship with God. In fact, it is entirely possible that those who search for something more than Jesus do so because they have never truly met Jesus. When you meet Jesus, you don't want anything more than Him.

**Read Matthew 7:21-23. Is Jesus real to you? How do you know?**

It is not enough to know about Jesus. Faith in Christ is not just an accumulation of knowledge about Him. People who have been born again spend time with Jesus because they want to know His heart. True intercessors talk to and listen to God because they want to grow in their relationship with Him and do His will.

*You'll never be an intercessor without*
*spending time in God's presence.*

**What are some activities you are tempted to choose over spending time with God?**

What is the danger in those temptations?

Being known as a *friend of God* requires being wise with our time. Your time is a limited resource that you are asked to allocate each day. Friendship grows through time and regular intimacy, so it's worth looking at your schedule to see where your time goes. A friend of God who is growing in faith and interceding for others knows God—because he or she spends time with Him.

# AN INTERCESSOR STANDS IN THE GAP

Read Genesis 18:20-33. What did Abraham step forward to ask God?

How would you characterize Abraham's question of God in this situation? (Circle all that apply.)

impertinent    prideful    courageous    faithful

untrusting    trusting    humble    surprising

At first glance, it might seem like Abraham has some audacity to approach God so boldly. What we find, though, is that God wanted Abraham to press in to Him through prayer. God expected Abraham to dialogue with Him, and God expects the same of everyone Jesus has freed from sin's bondage.

What factors or feelings might have held Abraham back from interceding for people in this way?

What factors or feelings hold you back from interceding for revival on behalf of others?

Intercessors need to be strengthened, because they will . . .

    take the arrows of the enemy.
    bear the burden of people.
    fight the battle.
    risk their own lives.
    plead with God to move.
    keep the flame lit and stoke revival.

**In Isaiah 59, the nation was falling apart, and God was looking for someone tough to intercede. Read Isaiah 59:14–16. What kind of a culture did Isaiah experience and describe?**

In Isaiah's day, religious leaders were corrupt. Conspiracies were the natural order. The streets were filled with riots and violence. City officials were like wolves in sheep's clothing. The people were oppressing the poor and robbing others. Truth was being distorted. There was no justice.

**How did God respond?**

*When there is not an intercessor, God Himself becomes an Intercessor.*

Jesus took the form of human flesh and stood in the gap because God couldn't find an intercessor. He came because no human could adequately fulfill that role. We mess up. We are weak. We are insufficient and incapable. We falter and give up. We can't save ourselves.

So God sent His Son, Jesus. Jesus stood in the gap when He went to the cross. And He stands in the gap and intercedes for us still today.

**Read Hebrews 7:25. What does Jesus live to do?**

On your own, you can't be tough enough to take the arrows of the enemy, bear others burdens, fight the battle, risk your life, plead with God to move, keep the flame lit, and stoke revival. You can't be the intercessor the world needs, but Jesus can through you. When you don't know what to pray, the Spirit will intercede for you. When you don't know how to pray, the Holy Spirit does—and He will.

This is the gospel. We have One who intercedes for us. We have One who absorbed our sins. We have One who died in our place.

**Read Acts 1:8. What does the Holy Spirit intercede for you to receive?**

The key to a victorious Christian life is powerful prayer. God doesn't need your assistance. He doesn't need your input. He wants your attention. God is looking for men and women who will commit to pray. Will you stand in the gap and intercede for others to receive revival?

# SILENCE AND SOLITUDE
## SPIRITUAL PRACTICES

God continually pursues and revives you. He has forgiven you and brought reconciliation to your relationship with Him, and He wants to engage with you—to take that relationship as deep as you'll let Him. But you have to decide you want to engage with Him and develop that relationship. One critical way to do this is by implementing spiritual practices in your daily life.

So far in this study, you've learned about practices like silence and solitude, confession, repentance, fasting, and intercession. There are many more—Bible study, journaling, Scripture memorization, generosity, community, and Sabbath rest, just to name a few.

## 15 MINUTES

*This week, increase your practice of silence and solitude to fifteen minutes each day.*

*As you do, invite God to speak to you about the relationship between spiritual practices and revival in your life. Ask questions like: How should I fast? Who do I need to intercede for?*

*Use the blank space provided to journal what God reveals to you.*

*Scan athe QR code to hear guidance from Robby about spending time in silence and solitude.*

# SURRENDERING

# GROUP STUDY

## START

*Welcome everyone to session 4, "Surrendering." Before introducing session 4, take a few minutes to review session 3.*

Before we dig into this week's study on surrendering to God for revival, let's discuss what we learned last week. In our personal study, we discovered how fasting and interceding enable us and others to receive revival from God.

> **What did you learn about revival in your study of Daniel 10:2-14 and Genesis 18:16-33?**
>
> **What stood out to you as you began to connect spiritual disciplines like fasting and intercession with silence and solitude (pages 66-67)?**
> **How is your practice of silence and solitude going? What has been encouraging to you? Challenging?**

The spiritual disciplines we practice make room for the Spirit to do a work in us. And we all need that ongoing work to take place! We've identified some challenges that come in silence and solitude—those come because the work the Spirit is doing in us is great. It involves total surrender.

*To prepare for video session 4, pray that God will help each person understand and apply this truth:*

> Allow the Holy Spirit to work in you as
> you do ministry alongside Jesus.

# WATCH

*Use these statements to follow along as you watch video session 4.*

The Holy Spirit will be a Counselor to you.

**JOHN 14:26**

There is a fine line between glorifying God and glorifying self.

1. Don't let your charisma outperform your character.

2. Don't let your giftedness outpace your godliness.

3. Don't let fanfare overshadow your faithfulness.

Return to your first love.

**MATTHEW 11:28-30**

To access the teaching sessions,
use the instructions in the back
of your Bible study book.

# DISCUSS

*Use these questions and prompts to discuss the video teaching.*

In the introductory segment of the video, Robby named a few things he's learned about the Holy Spirit: He's not weird; He's a friend; He's a way better preacher, teacher, and leader than we'll ever be; and He is our Counselor.

Which of those lessons that Robby learned resonates with you? Why?

Read John 14:26. How does this help you understand the function that the Spirit fulfills in your life?

Why is it important that we ask the Spirit for wisdom and guidance as we seek to hear from God about revival?

The point was made in the teaching video that if we want to see God's agenda in and through us here on earth then we're going to have to listen to the guidance of the Holy Spirit. That's because there is a fine line between glorifying God and glorifying self.

What are some ways we might see the tension between glorifying God and glorifying self when God brings revival?

God is calling us to surrender ourselves completely to Him. Read the following verses and discuss what they teach us about total surrender:

Proverbs 3:5-6

Matthew 16:25

Luke 9:23

Romans 12:2

James 4:7

In and of ourselves, we don't have the capacity or the desire to surrender ourselves completely to God. As we learned in the video teaching, we are more prone to boast in ourselves than to be broken over our sin. It is easy for us to fall in love with the ministry of Jesus and out of love with the Jesus of our ministries. We are tempted to let the Bible become a tool instead of our treasure. In and of ourselves, we will let the Word of God bypass our heart.

How does the Holy Spirit help us combat those very human, very common temptations? What is our role in that?

Read Matthew 11:28-30. What does Jesus promise those who come to Him? Why is appealing about that to you?

Contrast the "yoke" of Jesus with the "yoke" we carry when we do not surrender ourselves completely to God.

As Robby explained in the teaching video, God can't fill a full vessel. As we come to Jesus in faith and take His yoke instead of the yoke of our human nature, He begins to fill us.

Have you completely surrendered to God? Are there any areas you're not allowing the Spirit to access? How can you know?

## CLOSE IN PRAYER

*Prayer Requests*

# To Be Filled

**If you had to choose one thing you could not live without, what would it be? Why?**

Most of us don't answer that question with the most obvious and important answer: oxygen. We actually can't live without oxygen, but many of us think first about our spouse, car, job, children, phone, or coffee. And the same principle is true in our spiritual lives. We can't live without the Holy Spirit, but many of us live every day like we don't need Him.

**In the day-to-day, how much do you rely on the power of the Holy Spirit?**

Think about what would happen if Jesus moved into your home today. Would you have more confidence? Would you be bolder in sharing your faith? Would you ask for help more often? If you are a believer in Christ, you have something just as good: the Holy Spirit lives in you.

## GOD GIVES HIS SPIRIT TO THOSE WHO ASK

**What do the following verses teach you about the Holy Spirit?**

1 Corinthians 12:12-13

Romans 8:9



Ephesians 1:13



Ephesians 5:15-18



Luke 11:13



*You were baptized with the Spirit at salvation.*
*You are filled with the Spirit after salvation.*


There is no two-step process to receiving the Holy Spirit. The Holy Spirit indwells you at salvation. And it is also true that you desperately need to be filled daily. Even though the Holy Spirit lives within you, you still need to be filled by Him. Ephesians 5:18 makes this clear. You are to "be filled by the Spirit." True revival depends on the work of the Holy Spirit. Looking at the original language of the New Testament we gain a deeper understanding of what this means. A better translation of "being filled" is "being controled" by the Spirit.

**BE FILLED IS:**
- An imperative command that requires continuous action
- For every Christian
- From God (In other words, you can't fill yourself with God's Spirit—God does it.)

Yesterday's filling is not good for today. Today's filling is not good for tomorrow. What does look like to continually seek the Spirit? What practices keep us in touch with His power?

Prayer precedes power. The disciples prayed for ten days, then they were filled with the Spirit (Acts 1–2). Later, when the believers raised their voices together to God in prayer, "the place where they were assembled was shaken, and they were all filled with the Holy Spirit and began to speak the word of God boldly" (Acts 4:31).

*Every great movement of God begins by not moving.*

## GOD'S SPIRIT FUELS THOSE WHO ASK

Has there ever been a time in your life when you would say you were on fire for Jesus? If not, why not? If so, what was different about you then?

In Luke 3:16, John the Baptist said that Jesus would "baptize you with the Holy Spirit and fire." In Acts 2:3, the Holy Spirit's coming manifested in a visible reality described as "flames of fire." What do these descriptions teach us about the Spirit's filling in our lives?

Scripture refers to the Spirit's presence on earth in terms of fire to reveal some important truths to us about His power in our lives. Fire is consuming. It emanates light and heat. It dispels darkness. When Jesus sets you on fire, everyone around you knows it.

*The Spirit's fire consumes.*

**If the Spirit's fire consumes, then why do we experience seasons when we would not describe ourselves (nor would others) as being on fire for Jesus?**

**What is the relationship between being on fire for Jesus and surrender?**

Fire burns at different levels of heat. It can exist as a small ember or large flame. It can be carefully contained or take off in any direction. The same is true of the Spirit's power in our lives.

The Spirit's fire consumes, but you can choose whether or not to surrender to it. Do you want to be full of self or do you want to be full of the Spirit? It's His power, but it's your choice.

**What do the following verses teach you about that choice? What are some ways you can reject the Spirit's consuming power?**

1 Thessalonians 5:19

Ephesians 4:30–31

**What can you infer about revival from these verses?**

The good news is the Spirit doesn't leave us. If you are a believer in Christ, you are "sealed" with the Holy Spirit living inside you (Ephesians 1:13). However, you can silence His voice and drown out His presence.

*The Spirit's fire can be quenched.*

**Based on Ephesians 4:31, are there some choices you've made recently that have grieved the Holy Spirit?**

The truth is, you can grieve the Spirit who dwells within you for years and not be aware of it. Take the first word listed in Ephesians 4:31—bitterness. Bitterness manifests itself in anger, annoyance, resentment, jealousy, impatience, and irritability. That means you grieve the Spirit and quench His power in your life when you . . .

hold resentment toward someone for something in the past.
lose your temper.
are jealous of another family member, church member, or church.
allow a political comment to make you lose your cool.
speak with a condescending attitude toward your spouse.
yell and fume as someone cuts you off in traffic.

And the list goes on and on.

**Read 1 Thessalonians 4:7-8. Why do those choices quench the Spirit's work in your life?**

The Holy Spirit is holy. Therefore, He can't work in unclean vessels. This is why we must surrender to the Spirit's work in our lives. He will not adjust to you—you must adjust to Him. He will not be coerced or manipulated. He won't be pushed or prodded.

Are your words and actions in the day-to-day primarily determined by other people or by the Holy Spirit in you? Why?

*It doesn't matter who you please*
*if you displease God.*

How can considering the ways we grieve the Holy Spirit be an act of surrender?

What would change in your life this week if you began to consider how you could live in step with the Spirit (Galatians 5:16)?

When we begin to consider how we're grieving the Holy Spirit, we'll have fewer arguments, divorces, addictions, road rages, fights, and church splits. It will change how we talk to our spouses, discipline our children, do our work, respond to our parents, drive our cars, and converse with our enemies.

If we worried about how the Holy Spirit of God responds to us as much as we worried about people, we'd walk in a supernatural power.

*When you start worrying about grieving*
*the Holy Spirit, it changes everything.*

# Without Limits

Because the Holy Spirit lives within us, we have the potential to do great things for God. If you are a believer in Christ, the same power that raised Jesus from the dead is at work in *you* (Romans 8:11). The same power that Jesus had to turn water into wine, multiply bread and fish to feed multitudes, walk on water, and perform miracles of healing is available to you.

It is available to you in its fullness, and it is also available for you to limit at will. God offers you the option of whether you will live in His power or yours.

**Reread 1 Thessalonians 5:19 and review this week's previous personal study. What has God taught you so far about stifling His Spirit?**

"Don't stifle the Spirit" is a command. The Greek word for "stifle" can mean put out, extinguish, quench, block, or neglect. God is telling us we should never think of neglecting His Spirit's power and work in our lives.

Stifling the Spirit is like of putting out a fire and removing any trace of its existence. At the moment of salvation, God lit a fire in your heart. You didn't start the fire, but you can stack the wood and fan it into flame. The intensity of the fire burning in your life is connected to your relationship with the Holy Spirit.

## WE QUENCH THE SPIRIT WITH LIMITATIONS ON GOD

**Have you ever heard of something happening in the church and thought, "That's not of God. There's no way God would do that"? Explain.**

Why are we prone to think spiritual movements we hear about are manipulated (at best) or completely false?

We should not blindly accept every spiritual movement as genuine revival. In fact, 1 John 4:1 instructs us to "test the spirits to see if they are from God" because there is falsehood among us. However, we also should not automatically view spiritual moments as disingenuous. When we do that, we are saying in effect that God can't do something.

Besides being unequivocally wrong, what is the problem with putting God in a proverbial box when it comes to revival?

Certainly "revival" can be the result of a manipulative program or plan produced solely by human effort. Equally true and vastly more applicable to believers in Christ is the truth that we can miss revival because our prayers are way too small.

*We limit God working in our lives by our unbelief.*

Read the following verses to note a few extraordinary things God has proven He can do.

Exodus 14:21

Numbers 22:28

Joshua 6:2-5,20

Joshua 10:12-13

How do stories like these challenge or encourage your faith?

Read Ephesians 3:20-21. What can God do? How does He do those things?

*God wants to take the ceiling of your
faith and make it the floor.*

How, then, should you respond to the truth of Ephesians 3:20-21?

Your expectations of God might quench the Spirit's work in your life. God can do more than we can even conceive of. Don't limit God with your small prayers. Don't limit God in your life with unbelief. William Carey, the father of missions, said it like this: "Expect great things; attempt great things" in relationship to God.[1]

What is one big thing you need to believe God will do in your life?

What is one big thing you need to believe God will do in the life of your family?

---

1.  William Carey, "Expect Great Things; Attempt Great Things," William Carey University, 1792, https://www.wmcarey.edu/carey/expect/expect.pdf.

What is one big thing you need to believe God will do in the life of your church?

Why does surrendering to God involve believing in Him for big things? When have you experienced the necessity of that concurrence?

Since God can do more than we can ask or imagine (Ephesians 3:20), He can certainly do much more than we are able. When we surrender our feeble plans to His sovereign authority and unlimited power, we make room for Him to work outside the realm of human standards. When we surrender to God, we invite Him to disrupt our usual ways to show us something unusual.

# WE QUENCH THE SPIRIT WITH FORMALITY AND ROUTINE

When you go join with your church for times of worship and Bible study, do you expect God to move in your life? Do you anticipate God will speak to you, or is "church" just another activity on the calendar? Why?

*Busyness may be the roadblock to God working in your life.*

Many of us are bound so tightly to our schedules that the Spirit doesn't step in because we make no time for Him. We have given Him no room to move. Every free moment we have is filled with phones in our hands or calls in our ears. We are quick to answer the phone when someone calls but are hesitant to answer the Holy Spirit when He whispers.

Read 1 Kings 19:11-13. When Elijah was exhausted from *doing,* what did he need to do to hear from God? How did God choose to speak to Elijah?

How are you making room for God to work in your life? What do you need to do to hear and answer God's whisper?

## WE QUENCH THE SPIRIT BY DISOBEDIENCE

Limiting God in unbelief is a sin (Hebrews 3:12). But that's not the end of the story. We can acknowledge our unbelief, hear God's voice, and be led by His Spirit (Mark 9:24). The busyness of formality and routine that prevent us from hearing God's voice is a sin (Proverbs 28:9). But we can enter into God's presence in stillness, hear His voice, and be led by His Spirit (Psalm 62:5). Disobedience to God's commands throughout Scripture is also a sin (John 14:15). And God wants us to acknowledge those sins so that His Spirit can lead us in the better way.

Read Proverbs 28:13. What two choices do you have regarding your sins? What are the effects of those two choices?

Why isn't confession of sins enough? What does it mean to renounce your sins?

**What sins are you concealing? Why?**

The gauge of spiritual maturity in your life is the duration between conviction of sin and confession of sin. The main way we put out the fire of God in our lives is when the Spirit points out a sin and we ignore it. If you are living in sin and shushing the Spirit, you are in great danger. You can only silence Him so many times before He stops speaking.

The devil wants you to believe you don't need to hear God's voice. He wants you to feel you don't need spiritual revival. He wants you to think you can live this life without God's power and direction. You *can't*.

The invitation God gives you is contained in two words: total surrender. Partial obedience is disobedience. Delayed obedience is disobedience. Ask the Holy Spirit, *What are you leading me to do today?* And do it now.

*You cannot surrender to God's movement in your life and also reject His revealed will.*

# GOING DEEPER
## WAITING

God works for those who will wait on Him (Isaiah 64:4). How long would you be willing wait for God to pour out His Spirit? Are you willing to say, "God I'm not going to move until you move in my life"?

## 20 MINUTES

*As a practical way of waiting on God, increase your time of silence and solitude this week to twenty minutes each day. As you do, try the 95/5 principle. Spend ninety-five percent of the time listening and five percent of the time talking. That means you'll spend nineteen minutes not saying a word. Then, for one minute, respond verbally to God. Use the following two prompts to guide your time:*

**Ninety-five percent** *Recognizing you can't be filled with God and full of self, invite God to reveal every area you need to surrender to Him.*

**Five percent** *Ask for a filling of His Spirit and to be set on fire for God.*

*Use the blank space provided to journal what God reveals to you.*

*The difference between you and the power of God is the distance between your knees and the ground.*

_Scan athe QR code to hear guidance from Robby about spending time in silence and solitude._

SESSION 5
_____

# BELIEVING

# GROUP STUDY

## START

---

*Welcome everyone to session 5, "Believing." Before introducing session 5, take a few minutes to review session 4.*

In our personal study last week, we discovered that we can limit God working in our lives when by our unbelief. God brings revival when we fully surrender ourselves to Him. Let's discuss together some of the insights we've gained.

> **What did you learn about revival in your two days of personal study?**

> **We were encouraged to extend our time of silence and solitude to twenty minutes per day this week! What has God been teaching you through this practice?**

> **What stood out to you as you considered the role of waiting for God to move in your life?**

When we decide not to move until God moves in our lives, we must also decide to move when God gives us a word. In this week's teaching, we'll see that faithfulness involves action.

*To prepare for video session 5, pray that God will help each person understand and apply this truth:*

> Get a word from God, believe it, and act on it.

# WATCH

*Use these statements to follow along as you watch video session 5.*

Faith is the conviction that God's Word is true and that by acting upon God's Word it will bring blessing in your life.

**EXODUS 17:12-13; HEBREWS 11**

Every need brings us closer to God and grows us in our faith.

Our faith is the lid and the limit of God's power in our lives.

**MARK 9:17-29**

To access the teaching sessions,
use the instructions in the back
of your Bible study book.

# DISCUSS

*Use these questions and prompts to discuss the video teaching.*

At the beginning of the video teaching, Robby asked "Do you have a word from God that you're by faith acting on and believing God for your life?" Do you?

Considering all we've learned in the study so far, what are some reasons a believer might not have a word from God that they're believing and acting on? Use the weekly titles as help to get your thoughts going!

The title of this week's study is "Believing." In the teaching video, we learned that believing involves faith and faith involves action.

Read Exodus 17:12-13. What were Moses, Joshua, Aaron, Hur, and all of Israel believing about God?

What actions were required by each to demonstrate that belief?

Name one thing you believe about God. Now name an action that demonstrates that belief.

Why are faithful actions a necessary aspect of true belief?

The heroes of the faith described for us in Hebrews 11 illuminate the point. They are not remembered simply because they declared some measure of belief in God. They are remembered because their belief in God compelled them to act in extraordinarily faithful ways. That's what true faith does—it prompts us to act in ways that demonstrate our belief.

Read James 2:18-26. What is wrong with the idea that a person can live however he wants as long as he believes Jesus is Savior and Lord?

Reread verse 26. We've been seeing the importance of both surrendering to the Spirit in our lives and faithful actions. How should we understand the connection between the Spirit, faithfulness, and revival? Can revival take place in our lives apart from the Spirit? Apart from faithfulness?

In the video teaching, Robby led us to consider the effect of belief in God's sovereignty over our lives and the world. He pointed out that if God is in control, then His supply for our need comes before our need for His supply. Every need, then, brings us closer to God and grows us in our faith.

Think of a specific need you have, whether it is physical, emotional, or spiritual. What do you believe about God in that need? What would it look like for you to act on what you believe about God in that need?

The Bible makes a connection between belief and blessing. The one who believes in Jesus "will have streams of living water flow from deep within him" (John 7:38). When we know and believe "the length and width, height and depth of God's love" (Ephesians 3:18), we find that He "is able to do above and beyond all that we ask or think according to the power that works in us" (Ephesians 3:20).

Robby talked about praying "Him-possibles." Name an impossible thing you are believing God for or want to begin believing God for. Pray together big prayers, knowing you have a big God and can anticipate Him working in your lives.

## CLOSE IN PRAYER

*Prayer Requests*

_____

_____

_____

# The Reality of Faith

"Don't tell me how it ends!" If you haven't said those words, you've heard them from someone else. When you're planning to see a movie and someone tells you how the story ends, you feel disappointed. Discovery is part of the fun. At the same time, you can still enjoy a movie even when you know how it ends. Spoiler alert: What makes a movie influential is not the end, it's the journey.

This is true of the Christian life too: You can enjoy the journey more because you know how it will end. What makes Christianity meaningful is not just getting to heaven when you die, it's experiencing the fullness of God while you're here on earth.

**In what ways are you experiencing God's fullness right now? Why is it important to recognize what God is doing in the middle of the journey?**

*You can know God personally.*
*You can hear Him today.*

## FAITH HEARS FROM HEAVEN

Read Hebrews 11:1–3. Name a few unseen spiritual realities you are certain about.

Why are you certain of these spiritual realities?

While the Old Testament certainly shows sin as a reality of the human condition, it also shows us sinful people can choose faith—and they have. That's the theme of Hebrews 11. Sinful people believed God's promises were true before anyone ever saw those promises fulfilled. God approved them because of that faith.

Hebrews 11 also presents to us other outcomes of faith. The KJV expresses one such outcome in this way: "For by it the elders obtained a good report" (v. 2).

Their "good report" is their testimony recorded for us in Scripture. It's the Spirit-given witness of God's work in their lives preserved for us today. The Spirit moved and offered them the word of the Lord (v. 3), and they responded with faith and obedience.

What do the examples in Hebrews 11 teach us about depending on the Spirit and the life of faith? Why should we trust and press into these "reports"?

What is an example of a Spirit-given "good report" in your life?

What do the following verses teach you?

Numbers 23:19

Psalm 119:160

Galatians 1:8-9

2 Peter 1:20-21

When we make time to hear from the Lord, in faith, we will hear from Him. And we can faithfully move forward in confidence because the Holy Spirit will never reveal something contrary to God's Word.

> **Read Hebrews 11:13,17-19. What outcome of faith should there be for those who receive a word from God?**

God's people saw Him move. They heard a word from God. God revealed truth to them and they staked their lives on it—even when it didn't make any earthly sense. Hebrews 11 points us to a group of men and women who, like Abraham, saw God's promise before they experienced it. They believed it before anyone else could see it. They didn't have a Bible. They didn't read a word about God— they heard a word from God.

## FAITH STANDS ON REVELATION

> **Read Mark 6:41-52. What should the disciples have learned about Jesus in verses 41-44?**

People clearly saw the miracle of the loaves and the fish. Can you even imagine what such an experience would do for your faith? And the object lesson didn't end there. Jesus instructed His disciples to gather up the leftovers before boarding a boat to cross the Sea of Galilee without Him.

After they'd been straining against the wind all night, Jesus came to them in another object lesson. He was walking on water, but they thought He was a ghost—and they were terrified. In the moment of their terror, Jesus spoke to them, got in the boat, and the wind stopped. The lesson continued as Jesus connected their lack of faith to something besides the reality of wind and illusion of ghosts.

**Describe the disciples' problem in verse 52.**

Each disciple had a basket of bread at his feet, and those baskets were reve-latory. Jesus was teaching them about Himself. As they fed thousands and then loaded leftovers into the boat, they saw evidence that Jesus is the Messiah. This demonstrated Jesus can handle any situation that arises. Still, they panicked, because they had little understanding of who Jesus is and what He can do.

**We don't carry around baskets of leftovers, but we do have something even better—we have the revelatory Word of God at our fingertips. Read Romans 10:17. What is the connection between God's Word and your faith?**

*You can't trust Someone you don't know.*

Your faith doesn't rest on your resolve or willpower to believe; it rests on your understanding of who Jesus is. Faith isn't grasping into the unknown or unseen realm that is beyond your understanding. Faith is your response to a clear word from God. This is why Bible study matters. When you know the Bible, you know Jesus. And when you know Jesus, your faith becomes revelatory too.

# FAITH DEMANDS ACTION

Read Hebrews 11:17–38. What actions here stand out to you as most personally encouraging or challenging? Why?

In one sentence, summarize this section of Hebrews 11.

These men and women named in Hebrews 11 are not remembered for what they believed; they are remembered for what they did—for the lives their belief compelled them to live. You are not all that different than them. You have the same opportunity to be faithful. While the results might not be as "big," we don't evaluate the outcome of our lives of faith, our Father in heaven does.

*Faith is the conviction that God's Word is true and that by acting on His Word, you will receive blessing.*

What are some of the blessings you have received as you have acted in faith?

Does living a life of faith equal earthly comfort or success? Why?

Some men and women of faith came back to life after death. Others succumbed to death. Some were mighty in battle and experienced victory. Others were stoned or sawed in two. Some conquered kingdoms. Others were tortured.

Believing God in the fullness of who He is and acting in faith doesn't guarantee earthly comfort and success. Neither does it guarantee that the prayers of faithful people will be answered the way they want. In fact, the Bible is filled with prayers that weren't answered the way people hoped (Matthew 26:36-46; 2 Corinthians 12:7-10).

**What role did suffering and hardship play in the lives of those described in Hebrews 11?**

**Read Romans 5:3-5. Suffering is a part of the life of faith. Why, then, should you act on your faith?**

Being a Christian doesn't make you immune to pain and suffering. In fact, you may experience more suffering at times, but God promised a constant companion to walk through it with you. So don't doubt in the dark what God has revealed to you in the light. Run to Him. Trust Him to see you through it, and He will bless you in ways you would never otherwise comprehend.

**What does the reality of faith teach you about the reality of revival?**

**What is God calling you to stake your life on?**

# The Life of Faith

Today's session title might cause us to pause. That's because the life of faith is uncommon. The world is a complete mess, and unbelievers are not alone in that mess—we see it in the church too. Despite having the power of heaven at our disposal, many of us live defeated lives. We pray artificial prayers, void of any real hope for spiritual transformation. We settle for a synthetic Christianity that isn't Christianity at all.

*We need revival now more than ever before—*
*and we don't have time to waste.*

God has given us a way to overcome what is common; He has given us a way to overcome defeat. How can we enact that power? We can unleash the riches of heaven by living a life of faith.

## FAITH IS CONSTRUCTED WITH CONVICTION

Faith must have an object. We all believe in *something*.

> Think about a problem that concerns you. Now consider the objects of faith listed below. Circle any that you treat with personal conviction as worthy helps for addressing that problem.

intellect     expert opinions     physical strength

human strategies     good choices     money

Jesus     friendship     hard work

Those convictions aren't wrong. Certainly they are all helpful in solving various problems we face. But only Jesus is truly worthy of our *faith*. If we turn to anything or anyone else as our strongest conviction in life, our greatest victories will be short-sighted and short-lived, at best.

> **Read Mark 11:12-17,20-21. How did Jesus respond to people whose "faith" was in the wrong things?**

As Jesus approached the fig tree, He saw that the tree's leaves suggested fruit, but it hadn't produced. Jesus saw the tree as the representation of the hypocritical religious establishment that looked good from a distance but wasn't bearing fruit or being effective. As a result, Jesus cursed the fig tree.

Jesus didn't stop there. When He entered the temple, He saw price gouging, greed, and lack of reverence. He was filled with righteous rage and threw everyone out.

The message is loud and clear: Jesus deals with the hypocrisy of inauthentic faith. He doesn't demand perfection because we are all sinners, but genuine faith in Christ is constructed with conviction.

> **Read Mark 11:22-24. From Jesus's words here, how should the conviction of genuine faith in God manifest itself in our lives?**

> **Think again about the problem you're facing and the objects of your faith for addressing the problem that you identified on page 100. How do you need to apply Mark 11:12-24?**

In response to Israel's hypocrisy, Jesus cursed the fig tree and cleared the temple. Then He turned to His disciples and told them to keep trusting in God. In other words, don't let the lack of genuine faith you see around you—or even in yourself— diminish your expectations of God to move.

Jesus used hyperbole to make the point. Misplaced convictions of faith are mountainous obstacles standing in the way of true revival. *And,* Jesus is willing and able to remove those obstacles and bring revival if we will ask Him, believing He will.

## FAITH IS REALIZED THROUGH CONFESSION

It is possible to have conviction that only Jesus is truly worthy of your faith and still struggle with doubt. Have you ever experienced this? How so?

Doubt is an enemy to the life of faith. What are some practical ways we can fight doubts that come when we ask God to move mountains?

Circle the words *says* and *tell* in Mark 11:23-24.

"Truly I tell you, if anyone says to this mountain, 'Be lifted up and thrown into the sea,' and does not doubt in his heart, but believes that what he says will happen, it will be done for him. Therefore I tell you, everything you pray and ask for—believe that you have received it and it will be yours."

**MARK 11:23-24**

Our words carry great power. Verbal confession is a way of agreeing with God. It is an affirmation of what you believe—and it is a way to invite the Spirit to help you believe when doubts arise.

Faith is realized through the confession of biblical truths. When doubts arise, quote the Word of God.

**Consider the doubts we often think or verbalize. Then read the Scriptures listed and note the biblical truths that confront those doubts.**

I have failed miserably and am of no use to God.
*Ephesians 2:8-10*

There's no way this can turn out for good.
*Romans 8:28*

I can't do it.
*Romans 8:37*

I'm overwhelmed.
*1 John 4:4*

I'm living in defeat.
*Philippians 4:13*

I'm weak.
*2 Corinthians 12:9*

Without meaning to we sort our lives into two categories: possible and impossible. If you look at things from a human perspective, it will always seem impossible. But God only has one category: all things are possible.

How might speaking biblical truths aloud impact your faith going forward?

*Your internal dialogue affects the outcome of your life.*

Verbal confession can certainly be abused and often is. People often say things they don't mean. The moneychangers in the temple surely knew and quoted Scripture, but those truths didn't penetrate their hearts. And there is no magical "name it and claim it" guarantee, as some imagine. The authentic practice of faith isn't that easy. At the same time, words carry power. Speaking truth in our doubts can lead us to a deeper realization of faith.

**Based on today's study, what verbal confession do you need to make? Write it down and then say it out loud.**

## FAITH IS LIVED OUT WITH CERTAINTY

God makes promises that we can never experience with intellectual conviction and verbalized confession alone—genuine faith involves laying hold of the promises of God and applying them to our lives. This means we act on God's revealed truth by faith.

*Note the following two truths and corresponding promises, for example.*

TRUTH: Jesus died for the sins of the world (1 John 2:2).
PROMISE: Only those who have believed Christ's atoning sacrifice
by grace through faith experience eternal life (John 3:16).

TRUTH: The devil has been defeated on the cross (Colossians 2:15).
PROMISE: When we resist the devil, he will flee (James 4:12). Until we stand firm in the armor of God and embrace God's victory, he will continue to cause havoc in our lives (Ephesians 6:11–13).

**Read Mark 11:22–24 again. Identify God's revealed truth and how you must personalize and apply that truth to receive the promise.**

Truth:

Promise:

*When you get a word from God,*
*you need to stand on it.*

Our prayers must be appropriated by faith. Simple steps of faith release God's supernatural power in our lives.

You cannot experience revival apart from authentic faith in Jesus. Stop listening to the world. Have faith in God. Receive His Word of truth. Then stake your life on it as though heaven depends on it—because it does.

**What is a step of faith that you need to take?**

# GOING DEEPER
## PRAYING THE SCRIPTURE

Doubt undercuts faith and can sabotage the work of God in your life. That's why it's so important to allow the power of God's Word to construct your faith with conviction. The Bible doesn't offer explanations to cope with life's problems; it offers promises to cling to.

## 25 MINUTES

*This week as you increase your time of silence and solitude to twenty-five minutes each day, meditate on the promises of God. Listen to Him as He speaks to you from the following Scriptures or choose a few of your own. Use the blank space provided to journal what God reveals to you.*

For nothing will be impossible with God.

**LUKE 1:37**

Now if any of you lacks wisdom, he should ask God—who gives to all generously and ungrudgingly—and it will be given to him. But let him ask in faith without doubting.

**JAMES 1:5-6**

I will instruct you and show you the way to go; with my eye on you, I will give counsel.

**PSALM 32:8**

We know that all things work together for the good of those who love God, who are called according to his purpose.

**ROMANS 8:28**

*Scan athe QR code to hear guidance from Robby about spending time in silence and solitude.*

# SPREADING

# GROUP STUDY

## START

*Welcome everyone to session 6, "Spreading." Before introducing session 6, take a few minutes to review session 5.*

We've made it to the final session of *Revive Us.* This week, we'll complete our study in an exciting, forward-thinking way as we learn how the flame of revival fans the fame of revival. Before we jump in, let's review last week's study on believing in faithfulness.

> **What did you learn about revival in your study of Mark 11:12-24 and Hebrews 11?**

> **As you included the practice of praying the Scripture to your increased time of silence and solitude, how did God speak to you through His promises?**

When we define revival according to the purposes and promises of God found in His Word, prepare ourselves to receive those promises, surrender fully to the Spirit who fills us, and believe God by faithfulness, there will always be an effect. As God moves in us, He also begins to use us to impact the world.

> **What is one way God has been moving in you during this study, prompting changed behavior that others might notice?**

*To prepare for video session 6, pray that God will help each person understand and apply this truth:*

> When we die to ourselves, God begins
> to use us to impact the world.

# WATCH

*Use these statements to follow along as you watch video session 6.*

The motif of death in the Bible carries this message—death leads to life.

**JOHN 12:23-25**

Revival is a reawakening of something that is dead or dormant.

**MATTHEW 16:24; 2 CORINTHIANS 5:17**

God is looking for Spirit-filled men and women to change the world for Him.

**2 CHRONICLES 16:9**

To access the teaching sessions,
use the instructions in the back
of your Bible study book.

# DISCUSS

*Use these questions and prompts to discuss the video teaching.*

Robby said, "The flame of revival fans the fame of revival." What does that mean to you? Put it in your own words.

Read Psalm 34:8. What verbs are used? What do those particular verbs infer about the person who surrenders to the Lord in faithfulness?

Psalm 34 is about King David when he was in an especially difficult situation. The text makes it clear that David's relationship with God was not simply heady knowledge. David's relationship with the Lord had formed and grown through real world experience. He had tasted and seen for himself that God is good. Have you? There is no person on earth who can make you understand the goodness of God or impart to you the blessing of revival in Him. You have to experience Jesus for yourself.

Read Matthew 16:24-25 and John 12:23-25. Taken together, what do we learn from these two passages about what we must do to truly experience Jesus for ourselves?

What do you make of Jesus's statement in verse 25? How do the blessings of Jesus's kingdom exceed our own?

What promise is there for those who die to self and live for Christ?

Robby explained it this way: *The road to glory intersected with the cross at Calvary. Resurrection could only come from death.* That was true for Jesus and it is also true for everyone who chooses to follow Him. What God produces in the lives of those who lay down their earthly expectations to follow Him far exceeds our greatest imaginings. He brings new life in us, and the new life in us spreads to others. God uses new life in you to impact the world for His glory.

Read 2 Corinthians 5:17. In what ways are you different from who you were before becoming a follower of Christ?

How is the newness Paul describes in 2 Corinthians 5:17 a one time occurrence at the point of salvation? In what way is it also an ongoing process?

Robby explained the daily habit of denying self and experiencing new life in Christ. He said that every time self comes to mind, we must replace self with Jesus. That means letting go of the expectations we put on God and accepting His plans for our lives. It means asking the Holy Spirit to reveal self sufficiency, selfish pride, selfish agendas in our lives.

The flame of revival fans the fame of revival. But before we can see that happen—before we see revival in our homes, churches, communities, and world—it has to start in us.

God can do more in a moment than any man or woman can manufacture in a lifetime. What is something God has done in your life during this study? How will you faithfully believe in Him to continue that work?

# CLOSE IN PRAYER

*Prayer Requests*

_____

_____

_____

# A Message to Share

**As we enter the final week of our study, look back through these pages and identify one or two truths that have stood out to you.**

If you've made it this far, it's clear that you want to experience revival. And God wants that for you too. His aim is not simply for you to learn a few new truths—God wants you to experience the power of His Spirit in abundance every day.

*Revival starts with you, but it doesn't end there.*

**Why do defining, preparing, receiving, surrendering, and believing revival fall short if you never share what God has done with someone else?**

**Read Acts 1:8. For what purpose did God fill His disciples with His Spirit?**

God wants spiritual revival to take place in your life, *and* He wants to revive every person on the planet. The effects of believers defining, preparing, receiving, surrendering, and believing for revival are meant to extend beyond us. God fills us with His Spirit for global purpose—so that we will proclaim Him to a lost world.

# GOD'S SPIRIT COMPELS US TO SPEAK BOLDLY

The book of Acts is the sequel to the book of Luke. Luke the physician wrote both books, and Acts picks up right where the book of Luke ends. That's important, because Luke wrote about the power of the Holy Spirit described in Acts 1:8 more than once.

Eight times across the pages of the two books, Luke used the Greek word *pimplēmi*. In English we translate it as "filled with.'" Every time you see this word associated with the Holy Spirit, it is always followed by a bold proclamation of the Word.

**Read the eight instances of this word in Luke and Acts. Note who was filled with the Spirit and the purpose of that filling.**

Luke 1:13-17. _____ will be filled with the Holy Spirit (vv. 13-15), and he will _____ (vv. 16-17).

Luke 1:39-43. _____ was filled with the Holy Spirit (v. 41), and she exclaimed _____(v. 42).

Luke 1:67-68. _____ was filled with the Holy Spirit and _____.

Acts 2:2-4. _____ were filled with the Holy Spirit and _____.

Acts 4:7-10. _____ was filled with the Holy Spirit (v. 8) and _____(v. 10).

Acts 4:31. _____ were filled with the Holy Spirit and _____.

Acts 9:17-20. _____ was filled with the Holy Spirit (v. 17)

and _____(v. 20).


Acts 13:8-11. _____ was filled with the Holy Spirit (v. 9)

and _____(vv. 10-11).


**Based on these passages, how should the indwelling of the Spirit affect your life?**


The believer who is filled becomes a mouthpiece for the Spirit. When you're filled with the Spirit, you will direct attention to Jesus. Evangelism tools are helpful, but they're not the impetus for revival. When we seek the Lord fervently in prayer and follow the lead of His Spirit, we will be compelled to speak in ways that invite people to come and see what God is doing.


*A Spirit-filled believer will talk about Jesus.*


**Read Acts 17:1-7. What two ways did people respond when Paul and Silas proclaimed the name of Jesus in Thessalonica?**


**Why would Paul and Silas continue to proclaim Jesus when their lives were at risk?**


**Despite the opposition these early Christians faced, what effect did the indwelling of the Spirit have in and through their lives (v. 6)?**

Without a completed Bible, organized church services, conferences, revivals, resources, books, curriculum, tactics or techniques, the first century disciples turned the world upside down for Jesus. That's what happens when God's people do God's work in God's power for God's glory.

**When was the last time you talked to an unbeliever about Jesus?**

**Read 1 Corinthians 1:26-30. How is it possible for you to turn the world upside down for Jesus?**

God uses ordinary people to turn the world upside down. In fact, throughout Scripture we see that God uses our ordinariness to move His plan forward.'

We can devote ourselves to learning the strategies of evangelism. We can plan, prepare, read books, attend conferences, and gather knowledge—and we should. All of those efforts are helpful and good. At the same time, exactly zero of those evangelism strategies are primary. We *must* spend time praying and asking God to move.

**To this point, what has been your greatest focus in telling people about Jesus: strategizing and gathering knowledge or praying for God to move? Why?**

**What is the danger in strategizing for evangelism without praying for God to move?**

# ASK FOR A FILLING AND SPEAK BOLDLY

Read Matthew 26:69-70. Describe Peter's response to fear before the Holy Spirit came on him at Pentecost.

Read Acts 2:14-21. Describe Peter's response to fear after the Holy Spirit came on him at Pentecost.

Before Pentecost, Peter didn't have the courage to defend Jesus to a young servant girl as they sat around a fire. After Pentecost, Peter preached fearlessly in front of powerful people. Before Pentecost, Peter was a lamb. After Pentecost, Peter was a lion. Before Pentecost, Peter only wanted to talk about himself. After Pentecost, Peter couldn't stop talking about Jesus.

Let's dig a little deeper into Peter's story. Read Matthew 26:38-43 and Acts 1:13-14. What contrast in attitude and behavior do you find in the two passages?

We learned about this in week two of our study, and it is impossible to be reminded enough—when we pray honestly and humbly in accordance with God's character, purpose, and ultimate glory, He will revive us (page 43). And when God revives us, He fills us with His Spirit so we can boldly proclaim the name of Jesus. When we boldly proclaim the name of Jesus, revival spreads.

Let's take a look at one more example. Read Acts 4:8–21. What effect did Peter and John being filled by the Holy Spirit have in the following verses?

vv. 8–12:

v. 13:

v. 14:

vv. 16–18:

vv. 19–20:

v. 21:

Read Acts 4:23–33. What continued effects came as a result of the filling of the Holy Spirit?

vv. 24–28:

vv. 29–30:

v. 31:

vv. 32–33:

The disciples walked with Jesus in the flesh, yet they were empowered to spread the message of Jesus to the greatest extent when they, by prayer, walked with His Spirit. And we will experience the same empowering when we walk with the Spirit.

God wants to revive us, and He wants us to revive everyone around us. Are you ready? Prayerfully invite Jesus to fill you with the power of His Spirit and then let Him boldly speak through you. When the gospel spreads, revival comes.

*Let's ask God to fill us so we can
share Jesus without fear.*

# The Flame of Revival

Name one or more specific outcomes you'd like to see come about through revival . . .

in your personal life.

in your local church.

in your community, nation, and world.

Six weeks ago you may have opened this study book with hopeful expectation to experience revival. Since then, you've been digging into God's Word to better understand His heart for your life and the world. You've learned how God wants you to define spiritual revival. You've learned that He wants you to prepare, receive, surrender, and believe Him for the revival He brings. And now you're considering what it looks like for you to join Him in the spreading of revival.

At the same time, revival can't be scripted, even by the most spiritual, well-intentioned human beings. We only perceive what our senses detect, but God is always at work behind the scenes, writing a story we are prone to miss.

*God is working below the surface of your life to*
*work all things for our good and His glory.*

The salvation of a friend, the repentance of a family member, personal renewal of faith—whatever outcomes you might imagine in revival—God is ready, willing, and able to do more. Don't settle for the work of God to stop with what you've experienced or even what hopes you can verbalize. As God's people continue to prepare, receive, surrender, and believe Him for revival, the flame of revival will continue to spread.

Though we can't possibly identify the infinite outcomes God plans to bring about through the revival of His people, we can identify broader categories those outcomes fall within.

## UNITY

**Read Genesis 11:1-9. What outcome did God's people want to experience?**

People from all nations spoke the same language at one time. They gathered to build a city and a tower that would reach into the sky. They hoped for a revival of sorts—a unity of name and purpose. Only, the name and purpose they sought was self-activated and self-serving, creating themselves as an entity. So God came down, confused them with different languages, and then scattered them around the world.

**What work would God's people have been able to perceive that He was doing in verses 8-9? Choose all that apply:**

□ revealing His authority     □ causing dependence

□ punishing sin     □ teaching humility     □ changing plans

□ allowing struggle     □ other _____

It is likely that many of their perceptions were correct but didn't tell the whole story—not even close! God was at work in ways His people could not even imagine. To discover what God was doing behind the scenes in Genesis 11, fast forward two thousand-plus years to Pentecost (30 AD).

Pentecost is the Festival of Weeks. The word means fiftieth—it's seven weeks of seven days plus one. It's called the Festival of Firstfruits in Leviticus because it was in this time of celebration that Israel brought the first part of the harvest to God. Genesis 11 brings back together what Babel pushed apart.

**Read Acts 2:1-11. Contrast this passage with Genesis 11. What differences do you find?**

*The ministry of the Holy Spirit is never about confusion; it's always about clarity and unity.*

Babel was a group of people unified against their Creator, so God confused their language and scattered them. At Pentecost, these scattered and divided people were suddenly in the same place, hearing the same words together. The primary miracle of Pentecost is not that the people spoke in tongues—it's that they heard those spoken words in their own languages. God empowered His people for service in His kingdom to make His name known.

The sin of Babel was that God's people wanted their names to be known. The blessing of Pentecost is that God's name was exalted.

**When are you tempted to spread your own name and renown? What are some specific ways that temptation plays out?**

**Why does selfishness cause disunity in the church?**

Spreading the fame of self is both an individual and corporate temptation—it always has been. God's people, even while praying for revival, can be tempted to focus on self—the fame of a pastor, the numerical growth of a congregation, a fun and exciting reputation within the community, and the list goes on.

The fame of self always causes disunity, which brings physical, emotional, and spiritual consequences. However, what is impossible in our strength is possible with God. When revival occurs, He gets the glory, not us. This is for our good! The Spirit unifies us under God's name and for His kingdom purpose.

## POWER

Look back over the outcomes of revival you listed on page 120. Write a *U* beside any that could be categorized as effects of unity in the Spirit. Write a *P* beside any that could be categorized as effects of the Spirit's power.

When we look back at the very first Passover and forward to Pentecost, we learn more about the overarching outcomes of revival. To redeem His people from the bondage of Pharaoh, God instructed them to kill an unblemished lamb and put the blood on the doorposts of their homes. This served as a sign of which houses to pass over as God executed judgment on the gods of Egypt.

Look back over the description of Pentecost on page 122. What does the word *Pentecost* mean?

Fifty days after the first Passover, which began Israel's escape from captivity, Moses ascended Mount Sinai to receive the law. So the Jews remember Pentecost as God coming down and giving the law to Moses.

However, when Moses came down from the mountain, he found the people worshiping a golden calf. Outraged, Moses took the idol, burned it, crushed it into powder, and made the people drink it (Exodus 32:20).

Read Exodus 32:27–28. What else would Israel remember about the first Pentecost?

The judgment of God fell on Israel in no uncertain terms. Yet, as with the Tower of Babel in Genesis 11, God was at work beyond what His people could perceive. He was writing a story that they had, so far, missed.

In the New Testament, Jesus died on Passover. The same day Moses saved the people from the bondage of Egypt by sacrificing a spotless lamb, God saved humankind from the bondage of sin by sacrificing His sinless Son on a cross.

**Read Acts 2:37-41. What specific outcome of the Spirit's power occurred fifty days later at Pentecost?**

Examine the chart to understand these parallel contrasts in the Old and New Testaments.

| | EXODUS 12; 31:18–32:35 | ACTS 2:37-41 |
|---|---|---|
| **PASSOVER** | Israel sacrificed unblemished lamb and freed from captivity | Jesus sacrificed His life to redeem all who believe. |
| **PENTECOST** | God came down to give Moses His law on stone tablets. | God came down on by His Spirit to write the law on our hearts. |
| | Moses came down to find people worshiping a golden calf. Three thousand people died in judgment. | People worshiped God and three thousand received life and the Spirit. |

**Describe how was God at work beyond what His people could perceive.**

This is what God does! He re-rights the wrongs of humankind. He makes all things new. He exerts His power to redeem and restore us from the devastating loss our sins have caused.

Just like at Babel, God rewrote the story of the judgment of three thousand after the first Pentecost. And He wants to write a new story in our lives now.

**The outcomes of revival are the spread of the Spirit's unity and power. In what situations do you need to experience unity in the Spirit? In what situations do you need to experience the power of the Spirit?**

**Is it possible to be a part of the spreading of revival apart from the unity and power of the Spirit in your own life? Why or why not?**

**Reread Acts 2:37–41. What do you need to do to experience the power of revival in your life?**

*You have a choice to accept the message or reject it.*

The outcome of the Spirit's power for repentance, redemption, and restoration is available to every person in Christ. We each have personal responsibility in choosing to accept it, though. God is ready to spread the flame of revival through the unity and power of His Spirit. Will you let it spread through you?

# GOING DEEPER
## MORE OF GOD

Maybe we don't even recognize it, but so often we strategize just like God's people at Babel (Genesis 11) and around the fire at the foot of Mount Sinai (Exodus 32). Instead of desperately seeking more of God, we try to give people more of ourselves. And in those strategies, we will never experience the revival God longs to bring. Our human efforts are entirely insufficient. We are incapable of attaining and spreading the Spirit's unity and power. We need more of God.

How do we receive more of God? That's what these times of silence and solitude have all been about. Let's enter into this week's commitment of thirty minutes before the Lord, not as an end to the study, but as the beginning of a way of relating to God that knows no earthly end.

## 30 MINUTES

*This week as you spend time in silence and solitude before the Lord, consider this one question:*

> *If the spread of revival in your life, church, and community depended on your prayers, your faith, and your obedience, would revival occur?*

*Invite the Lord to speak to you plainly about how He wants to give you more of Himself in your prayer life, faith, and obedience going forward from these six weeks in the Revive Us study. Use the blank space provided to journal what God reveals to you.*

*Scan athe QR code to hear guidance from Robby about spending time in silence and solitude.*

# REVIVE US

A HEART READY FOR REVIVAL

## LEADER GUIDE

# TIPS FOR LEADING A
# SMALL GROUP

*Follow these guidelines to prepare for each session.*

## PRAYERFULLY PREPARE

**REVIEW.** Review the personal studies and group questions ahead of time.

**PRAY.** Be intentional about praying for each person in the group. Ask the Holy Spirit to work through you and the group discussion as you point to Jesus each week through God's Word.

## MINIMIZE DISTRACTIONS

Create a comfortable environment. If group members are uncomfortable, they'll be distracted and therefore not engaged in the group experience. Plan ahead by considering these details:

seating

temperature

lighting

food or drink

surrounding noise

general cleanliness

At best, thoughtfulness and hospitality show guests and group members they're welcome and valued in whatever environment you choose to gather. At worst, people may never notice your effort, but they're also not distracted. Do everything in your ability to help people focus on what's most important: connecting with God, with the Bible, and with one another.

## INCLUDE OTHERS

Your goal is to foster a community in which people are welcome just as they are but encouraged to grow spiritually. Always be aware of opportunities to include any people who visit the group and to invite new people to join your group. An inexpensive way to make first-time guests feel welcome or to invite someone to get involved is to give them their own copies of this Bible study book.

# ENCOURAGE DISCUSSION

A good small group experience has the following characteristics:

**EVERYONE PARTICIPATES.** Encourage everyone to ask questions, share responses, or read aloud.

**NO ONE DOMINATES—NOT EVEN THE LEADER.** Be sure that your time speaking as a leader takes up less than half of your time together as a group. Politely guide discussion if anyone dominates.

**NOBODY IS RUSHED THROUGH QUESTIONS.** Don't feel that a moment of silence is a bad thing. People often need time to think about their responses or to gain courage to share what God is stirring in their hearts.

**INPUT IS AFFIRMED AND FOLLOWED UP.** Make sure you point out something true or helpful in a response. Don't just move on. Build community with follow-up questions, asking how other people have experienced similar things or how a truth has shaped their understanding of God and the Scripture you're studying. People are less likely to speak up if they fear that you don't actually want to hear their answers or that you're looking for only a certain answer.

**GOD AND HIS WORD ARE CENTRAL.** Opinions and experiences can be helpful, but God has given us the truth. Trust God's Word to be the authority and God's Spirit to work in people's lives. You can't change anyone, but God can. Continually point people to the Word and to active steps of faith.

# KEEP CONNECTING

Think of ways to connect with group members during the week. Participation during the group session is always improved when members spend time connecting with one another outside the group sessions. The more people are comfortable with and involved in one another's lives, the more they'll look forward to being together. When people move beyond being friendly to truly being friends who form a community, they come to each session eager to engage instead of merely attending.

When possible, build deeper friendships by planning or spontaneously inviting group members to join you outside your regularly scheduled group time for activities, meals, group hangouts, or projects around your home, church, or community.

# DEFINING

## KEY SCRIPTURE

Exodus 33:18

Psalm 46:10

John 1:14

## SESSION OUTLINE

Revival is a heightened awareness of the presence of God.
Before we can have this intimacy with God we have to know Him personally.
Before we can experience revival we must know Jesus.

## BEFORE THE SESSION

1. Review the group content as well as the video teaching session.
2. Read and review the Scriptures, making your own observations.
3. Decide whether you're going to watch the video teaching sessions together or if you want group members to watch them prior to the group meeting. Each video is around ten to fifteen minutes long.
4. Pray for all group members by name.
5. Review the questions in the Start and Discuss sections. Feel free to adjust or adapt the questions provided to better fit the members of your group.

## DURING THE SESSION

1. Make sure everyone is acquainted with one another. Consider sharing names and brief information so everyone feels welcomed and included.
2. People will have different ideas about what revival is—most more biblical, some more cultural—this session is an opportunity to level set and have the same working definition.
3. Highlight the personal as well as the corporate nature of revival.
4. Be sensitive to those for whom this is their first Bible study experience.
5. Introduce the silence and solitude exercise in the Going Deeper section. Entourage your group that participating in this exercise each week will help them get the most out of this study.
6. Consider breaking up into smaller groups for prayer support and accountability.
7. Close in prayer.
8. Remind them to complete the two Personal Studies and the Silence and Solitude exercise section before the next meeting.

## AFTER THE SESSION

Consider meeting in groups of two or three to discuss and review the guided reading. Here are a few questions to ask during that time. Alternately, you might consider sending these questions to the group in a text or email to consider on their own.

Which definition of revival resonated most with you?

What is the most significant takeaway from the first week of study?

What about this study was new or challenging to you?

## NOTES

# PREPARING

## KEY SCRIPTURE

Psalm 139:23-24

Proverbs 27:17

Galatians 6:1-2

James 5:16

## SESSION OUTLINE

1. Are you the blood clot to revival coming to your home, your church, and your community? Explain.
2. Repentance is change in one's mind about sin that leads to a change of action in one's life.
3. Three Steps to Repentance:
   i.   Acknowledge there is a God who knows what's best for you.
   ii.  Confess that sin to God.
   iii. Return to God.
4. Repentance is a lifestyle.

## BEFORE THE SESSION

1. Review the group content as well as the video teaching session.
2. Read and review the Scriptures, making your own observations.
3. Spent some time preparing your heart and repenting yourself.
4. Pray for all group members by name.

Review the questions in the Start and Discuss sections. Feel free to adjust or adapt the questions provided to better fit the members of your group.

## DURING THE SESSION

1. Make sure any newcomers are acquainted with everyone and welcomed into the group.
2. Recognize that this week's topic might be one those in your group haven't thought about and might be uncomfortable talking about, but repentance is essential to the Christian life and to spiritual vitality.
3. Ask about everyone's experience with the Going Deeper exercise.
4. Be willing to talk about your own sin in the group meeting because it will be key to helping others open and up and share theirs. Be careful to do this in a way that doesn't turn into storytelling about how bad we were but rather about how God has delivered us.
5. Close in prayer.
6. Remind them to complete the two Personal Studies and the Going Deeper section before the next meeting.

## AFTER THE SESSION

Consider meeting in groups of two or three to discuss and review the guided reading. Here are a few questions to ask during that time. Alternately, you might consider sending these questions to the group in a text or email to consider on their own.

In the group Robby introduced In the session Robby spoke about the Ignatian Examen, which is an exercise of identifying consolations and desolations—things that draw you to God and things that draw you away from God during the day. What might it look like for you to do this?

What is the "blood clot" that's keeping you from spiritual vitality?

## NOTES

# RECEIVING

## KEY SCRIPTURE

Mark 1:35-38

Isaiah 57:15

Psalm 46:10

## SESSION OUTLINE

1. We all need a place where we can meet with God.
2. God is always speaking to us. Are we listening?
3. Every great movement of God begins with not moving.

## BEFORE THE SESSION

1. Review the group content as well as the video teaching session.
2. Read and review the Scriptures, making your own observations.
3. Spent your own time in silence and solitude so that you can talk about your experience with the group and encourage their growth in this practice.
4. Pray for all group members by name.
5. Review the questions in the Start and Discuss sections. Feel free to adjust or adapt the questions provided to better fit the members of your group.

## DURING THE SESSION

1. Get the group talking about their own spiritual practices. There will likely be many different starting points that and is totally okay.
2. Highlight that receiving is about hearing from God and putting it into practice. This is an essential aspect of personal and corporate revival.
3. Point out that all of us have a tendency towards action, but sometimes the best thing for us to do might be to be still before God and hear from Him.
4. Walk through the exercise on Psalm 46:10 that Robby introduced in the group study video.
5. Close in prayer.
6. Remind them to complete the two Personal Studies and the Going Deeper section before the next meeting.

## AFTER THE SESSION

Consider meeting in groups of two or three to discuss and review the guided reading. Here are a few questions to ask during that time. Alternately, you might consider sending these questions to the group in a text or email to consider on their own.

Do you have a place where you meet regularly with God? If so, why is that place important to you? If not, where might be a place you can go?

What is going on in your heart when you're not prioritizing being alone with God?

What connection is there between spending time in silence and solitude before the Lord and becoming a humble and contrite person?

## NOTES

# SURRENDERING

## KEY SCRIPTURE

John 14:26

Matthew 11:28-30

## SESSION OUTLINE

1. The Holy Spirit will be a Counselor to you.
2. There is a fine line between glorifying God and glorifying self.
    i.   Don't let your charisma outperform your character.
    ii.  Don't let your giftedness outpace your godliness.
    iii. Don't let fanfare overshadow your faithfulness.
3. Return to your first love.

## BEFORE THE SESSION

1. Review the group content as well as the video teaching session.
2. Read and review the Scriptures, making your own observations.
3. Take the content and apply it to your own life. What are you surrendering as you study revival?
4. Pray for all group members by name.
5. Review the questions in the Start and Discuss sections. Feel free to adjust or adapt the questions provided to better fit the members of your group.

## DURING THE SESSION

1. Realize that surrender is difficult for people and does not come naturally but can be done when we partner with the Holy Spirit.
2. Ask people about their experience with the Holy Spirit. He is God and should be relied on and sought like God the Father and God the Son.
3. Talk about the fine line between glorifying God and glorifying self and how surrender is a path to finding more of God and less of yourself.
4. Be willing to ask people to share things they have not surrendered to God.
5. Close in prayer.
6. Remind them to complete the two Personal Studies and the Going Deeper section before the next meeting.

## AFTER THE SESSION

Consider meeting in groups of two or three to discuss and review the guided reading. Here are a few questions to ask during that time. Alternately, you might consider sending these questions to the group in a text or email to consider on their own.

> Have you completely surrendered to God? Are there any areas you're not allowing the Spirit to access? How can you know?

> How has your practice of silence and solitude been helping you know God better?

> Spend a few moments in prayer surrendering to God and giving Him space to work in your heart and life.

## NOTES

# BELIEVING

## KEY SCRIPTURE

Exodus 17:12-13

Hebrews 11

Mark 9:17-29

## SESSION OUTLINE

1. Faith is the conviction that God's Word is true and that by acting upon God's Word it will bring blessing in your life.
2. Every need brings us closer to God and grows our faith.
3. Our faith is the lid and limit of God's Power in our life.

## BEFORE THE SESSION

1. Review the group content as well as the video teaching session.
2. Read and review the Scriptures, making your own observations.
3. Pray for all group members by name.
4. If you are planning to meet beyond this study determine what you will study next.
5. Review the questions in the Start and Discuss sections. Feel free to adjust or adapt the questions provided to better fit the members of your group.

## DURING THE SESSION

1. Establish what we mean by "believing," which is having faith that what God is doing is real and will continue.
2. Point out that all of us have a word from God in the Scriptures and can hear from Him in prayer as well. Believing involves seeking God in faith.
3. Discuss the connection between faith and belief. Our faith demonstrates our belief and our beliefs support our faith.
4. Talk about how God being sovereign and good should lead us to trust Him.
5. Close in prayer.
6. Remind them to complete the two Personal Studies and the Going Deeper section before the next meeting.

## AFTER THE SESSION

Consider meeting in groups of two or three to discuss and review the guided reading. Here are a few questions to ask during that time. Alternately, you might consider sending these questions to the group in a text or email to consider on their own.

Do you have a word from God that you're by faith acting on and believing God for your life?

Discuss how our beliefs about God are connected to our actions

Name an impossible thing you are believing God for or want to begin believing God for. Share it with another believer and pray about it together.

## NOTES

# SPREADING

## KEY SCRIPTURE

John 12:23-25

Psalm 34:8

Matthew 16:24

2 Corinthians 5:17

2 Chronicles 16:9

## SESSION OUTLINE

1. The motif of death in the Bible carries this message—death leads to life.
2. Revival is a reawakening of something that is dead or dormant.
3. God is looking for Spirit-filled men and women to change the world for Him.

## BEFORE THE SESSION

1. Review the group content as well as the video teaching session.
2. Read and review the Scriptures, making your own observations.
3. Since this is the last session in this study, decide how you want to end this study experience.
4. Pray for all group members by name.
5. Review the questions in the Start and Discuss sections. Feel free to adjust or adapt the questions provided to better fit the members of your group.

## DURING THE SESSION

1. The point of revival is not the revival itself, but what happens after. When God moves in our lives, we are not mean to stay in one place.
2. Point out that other great revivals have led to mass movements of evangelism and faith.
3. This session and this study are not a completion or an end point but a jumping off point.
4. Remind the group that God can do more in a moment than we can in a lifetime so it is always right to expect God to do big things.
5. Thank the group for participating in the study and communicate what you will be studying next.
6. Close in prayer.
7. Remind them to complete the two Personal Studies and the Going Deeper section before the next meeting.

## AFTER THE SESSION

Consider meeting in groups of two or three to discuss and review the guided reading. Here are a few questions to ask during that time. Alternately, you might consider sending these questions to the group in a text or email to consider on their own.

> How is the newness Paul describes in 2 Corinthians 5:17 a one time occurrence at the point of salvation? In what way is it also an ongoing process?

> What is the most significant takeaway from this study?

> How will you fan the flame of revival in your own life?

## NOTES

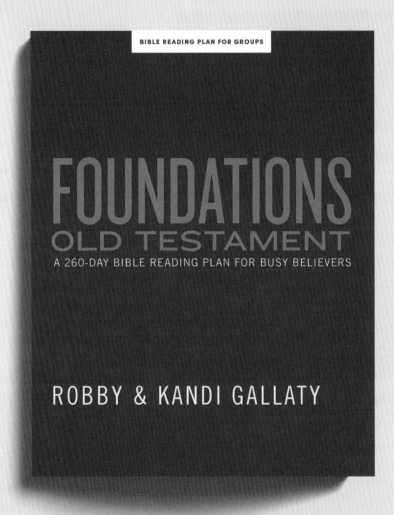

# Can it happen again?

Throughout the church age, revivals have sparked like wildfires in an ancient forest, beginning where it's least expected, gaining momentum, and then suddenly flaming out as quickly as it started. Is there a way to start one or fuel the flames once it's begun?

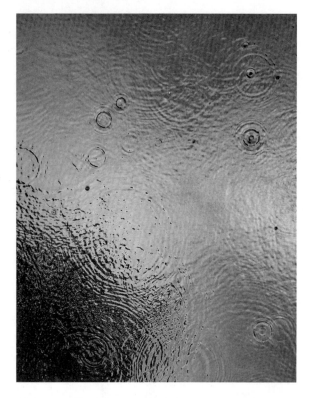

## ADDITIONAL RESOURCES

**eBOOK**
Bible Study eBook with Video Access

005847265 **$19.99**

*Price and availability subject to change without notice.*

While we can't orchestrate a revival on our own, we can request it and be ready when God chooses to answer that prayer.

This six-session study will help:

- Learn what revival means in the life of a Christian and a church.
- Petition God to see His work move forward in the world.
- Prepare yourself to be used by God for His work.
- Cultivate lasting spiritual habits that lead to long-term spiritual vitality.

Studying on your own?

To enrich your study experience, be sure to access the videos available through a redemption code printed in this Bible Study Book.

Leading a group?

Each group member will need a *Revive Us Bible Study Book*, which includes video access. Because all participants will have access to the video content, you can choose to watch the videos outside of your group meeting if desired. Or, if you're watching together and someone misses a group meeting, they'll have the flexibility to catch up.